CITY FISHING

Richard Chiappone, Jerry Dennis, Ian Frazier,
Pete Fromm, Paul Guernsey, J.H. Hall, Dave Hughes,
Nick Lyons, O. Victor Miller, Seth Norman,
James Prosek, Charles Rangeley-Wilson,
Jon Rounds, Art Scheck, Paul Schullery

STACKPOLE
BOOKS

Published by
STACKPOLE BOOKS
5067 Ritter Road
Mechanicsburg, PA 17055
www.stackpolebooks.com

Printed in the United States of America

Cover design by Caroline Stover
Cover photograph by Mark Allison

10 9 8 7 6 5 4 3 2 1

First edition

Library of Congress Cataloging-in-Publication Data
City Fishing/Richard Chiappone...[et al.].--1st ed.
    p. cm.
  ISBN 0-8117-0357-6
  1. Fishing--United States. I Chiappone, Richard.

SH463.C48 2002
799.1'09173'2--dc21   2001049839

CONTENTS

BRIGHT FISH, NICE CITY
J.H. Hall
1

URBAN GUERRILLA ANGLING
Seth Norman
11

RIVERS IN EXILE
Paul Schullery
19

ON URBAN SHORES
Ian Frazier
25

THE CHUBS
Richard Chiappone
35

ÎLE DE LA CITÉ AND
PARIS FISHING
James Prosek
52

THE FINE ART OF HUDSON
RIVER FENCE FISHING
Nick Lyons
62

FISHING THE JAM
Jerry Dennis
73

HERMAPHRODITES TO DRIES
Dave Hughes
80

MANHATTAN ODYSSEY
Paul Guernsey
93

HOLY WATER
Art Scheck
104

DOWNTOWN STRIPERS,
OAKTOWN ANGST
Seth Norman
116

THROUGH THE ICE
Pete Fromm
126

TROUT WITHIN THE M25
Charles Rangeley-Wilson
139

UNMEASURED CAVERNS
O. Victor Miller
151

FAREWELL GRAYLING
Paul Schullery
169

STONECATS IN THE
SUSQUEHANNA
Jon Rounds
176

Bright Fish, Nice City

J. H. Hall

In the fall of 1986 our Trout Unlimited chapter decided to clean the west bank of the Kennebec River below the Edwards Dam. Though few of us ever fished that section—it was in the middle of Augusta, Maine—our chapter bore the river's name, and we felt obligated to tidy up her much sullied shores.

The Kennebec has a long, storied, and somewhat sordid history. Over the centuries it has served as a source of food, a transportation route, a conduit for logs, a power source, a sewer, and a dump. But in the last decade the log drives had ended, pollution had been reduced, and the river was coming back to life. Amazingly, it still held fish.

It was a cloudy, cool October day when we arrived. The river's bank was a slippery mix of ledge and mud littered with tires, bottles, cans, grocery carts, assorted auto parts, coils of wire, and other unidentifiable pieces of scrap metal—several truckloads of material. The tide was low, and even as we removed the most recent layer of debris, we could see intriguing wakes at the shallow outlet of Bond Brook. The river was known to have a small run of Atlantic salmon of very controversial lineage. Native fish?

Penobscot strays? Escapees from a coastal aquaculture operation? People could not agree, but every fall a few dozen fish would stubbornly ascend the Kennebec until they hit the Augusta dam, at which point they would turn left into Bond Brook. A few people actually fished for them, but fishing in downtown Augusta had never appealed to me.

A decade earlier I had devoted a couple of seasons to the pursuit of Atlantic salmon in Downeast Maine. I never caught one. The closest I came was finding a prehistoric fishing site on the banks of the Machias River. On the basis of the plummet and projectile points I recovered, the state archeologist determined the site was last occupied about three thousand years ago—a really extreme example of "You should have been here yesterday." But that experience at least taught me what a salmon river ought to look like, and it did not look like the Kennebec in downtown Augusta.

Also, I had once seen a slide show by a very famous fishing author on "His Majesty," *Salmo salar,* filmed in England: gorgeous shots of lush green countryside, meandering streams, gleaming salmon, gillies (quite nattily attired), castles, and aristocrats—in other words, nothing whatsoever like Augusta. A slide show of salmon fishing in Augusta would feature the underbellies of two rusty bridges, the abandoned Edwards Mill, the backside of downtown Augusta, parking lots, old buildings, an adult video store, a seedy bar, a soup kitchen, and not a single aristocrat, just a few locals down on their luck. And to fully capture the flavor of the local fishing culture, there would have to be at least one unsavory character peering down from the Bond Brook bridge, an empty grocery cart in one hand, a length of rope in the other. (Though I've never seen the technique described in the fishing literature, as I understand it, the cart is lowered or dropped upside down onto spawning salmon. It at least sounds more sporting than snagging with treble hooks, another favored technique.) The sound track would include, not birdsongs, but loud traffic noises, sirens, horns, and booming subwoofers.

On the other hand, according to the experts in our TU chapter, those really *were* Atlantic salmon bulldozing around practically at our ankles, and after all those miles I'd driven to the Denny's, the Machias, and the Penobscot without even *seeing* a fish, didn't I deserve to catch at least one salmon in my life, even if it was under less than ideal circumstances? Wouldn't it be ironic, after all that effort, to find what I was looking for right under my nose, within three minutes of where I worked? It sounded like a metaphor for something, an important lesson, a learning experience. And who was I to say any piece of water was unworthy of my efforts? Who did I think I was, an aristocrat? No, I was, or fancied myself to be, a man of the people. I had even watched an adult video or two in my day. (But I had *not* rented them at seedy, inner-city joints. I had rented them—and only once or twice—in clean, wholesome places, which somehow elevated the adult video experience, and me, to a loftier moral plane.)

So the very next day after work, rod in hand, I returned to the cleanup site, which, despite the truckloads of debris we had removed, still did not look or smell particularly inviting. No matter. I donned waders, rigged up my rod just as if I'd been about to enter Cascapedia or Restigouche or Test. Fly selection presented a problem. Unable to locate my old Sucrets box of Atlantic salmon flies, I settled on a Warden's Worry, a local pattern that is quite effective on landlocked salmon, which are said to be genetically identical to the sea-run salmon. So why wouldn't it work? I used the same technique, too. After wading out and positioning myself as near to the heavy current as I dared, I made a series of quartering casts downstream and let the fly swing without stripping.

On my third cast I felt a heaviness, lifted the rod tip, and braced myself for the frantic run and the graceful leaps of "His Majesty," which, of course, never came. It was fall; this fish was

ready to spawn, and leaping high into the air was the last thing on
his mind. Instead, he managed a couple sluggish lunges, one or
two slow, arduous, carplike runs—more like walks than runs—
then burrowed into the current like a groundhog. A heavy fish,
ten to twelve pounds, I estimated, he meandered one way and
then the other, while I took line and gave line, all at a very
leisurely pace, salmon-fishing in slow motion. Which allowed
plenty of time, too much time, really, for me to savor the fact that
I was hooked up to my very *first* sea-run salmon, which should
have been a major milestone in anyone's fishing life.

In order to burn the moment into my memory—big mistake—I looked up and beheld the rusted underside of the abandoned railway trestle, Statler Tissue's unsightly posterior, more
debris along the far bank, the one we wisely hadn't even
attempted to clean. Wasn't that the front end of a '58 Ford Fair-
lane? My brother used to drive a car like that. Small world.

Meanwhile, my logy salmon was running out of steam. I had
decided ahead of time that I was going to tail that fish, because—
I'd seen the slide show—that was how you landed salmon. You
lipped bass; you netted trout; you tailed salmon. Those were the
rules. Besides, by then I had attracted a small audience of nonfish-
ermen peering hungrily down from the Father Curran Bridge,
and I wanted to show them, this is how you treat "His Majesty"
Salmo salar, with respect! You don't drop shopping carts on top of
him. No matter how hungry you are. If you want to eat salmon,
use your food stamps, not treble hooks! At this point, I'm afraid,
the "man of the people" had been possessed by the evil spirit of
an English viscount. (I blame that highfalutin slide show, which in
its own way was every bit as obscene as an adult video.)

Unfortunately, my tailing efforts were not going well. My
hands are not large; his tail was thick, wet, and slimy. Even a dark,
lethargic, twelve-pound salmon—he might have been fifteen—
was too much for my grip. The final stages of the struggle resem-
bled a rodeo event for kids. Finally, the hook simply fell out. I

pretended it was intentional. The fish held in the shallows around my ankles until, fully recovered, he swam slowly off. Any commentary from the onlookers above was fortunately lost in sounds of rush-hour traffic. That was enough for one afternoon. I waded ashore, and never fished there again, or had any desire to.

On the basis of that single experience, I decided that city fishing was simply not for me. Give me the real out-of-doors, the trees, the hills, the small wild fish, and keep your inner-city salmon. For thirteen years I never wet another line in Augusta. No matter how many rave reviews I read about the revitalization of the river or the return of the striped bass, and no matter how many boats I saw as I drove to work. I had my standards, and I stuck to them. Then in September of '99 something happened that made me reconsider my position: my friend Dan and I went west.

Dan also works in Augusta in sight of the Kennebec, which he also does not fish for the same reasons that I don't. We have similar standards, and for the most part, Dan and I like the same sorts of fishing. We part ways on salmon (which he pursues in Canada, not Augusta) and bass (which Dan, a New Englander and not a man of the people, disparages). But otherwise our fishing tastes are much alike. We prefer to wade medium-size streams for rising trout. No guided float trips for us.

One of our first stops out west was Poindexter Slough, a small spring creek on the outskirts of Dillon, Montana, that flows through a lush meadow before joining the more famous, more heavily fished Beaverhead. This was my third trip, but Dan's first. I had warned him in advance that this was not remote fishing. It is close to town; there is public access, a well-marked parking lot, heavily trod trails. Locals consider the Slough a nice place to walk, a picnic spot. The one blemish that I might not have mentioned, because I barely remembered it, was Interstate 15, an elevated four-lane highway that actually crosses the Slough. In fact, there's a rather nice, shaded pool beneath the overpass. Also, a train track runs along the other side of the meadow, but I've never seen an actual train use it. On the other hand, the flow of traffic on I-15 is as steady as the current of the stream and, therefore, hardly an intrusion, more like "white noise," a natural phenomenon. To me, the Slough is pastoral and serene, an oasis frequented by deer, ducks, wading birds, and songbirds. Beyond the highway, the sage-covered hills and open country stretch seemingly forever. And the stream itself—clear, sinuous, tranquil as a snake asleep on a lawn—is fertile and filled with vegetation and wild brown trout, some of which grow quite large.

Our first stop in Dillon was at the local fly shop. Though Dan and I disdain guides, we love free advice. The official word at the fly shop was, not much was hatching on the Slough. Use terrestrials. We loaded up on hoppers in various styles and sizes and headed for the Slough. (In our earlier, less prosperous days, we would have bought a single hopper and then hurried back to the motel to tie up replicas.) Riding out, I was optimistic. No hatches was great news. The first time I fished the Slough, too much was hatching. One evening I got caught in a biologic explosion; fish and bugs were everywhere. It was like an entomology exam, and I flunked. Maine fishing had not adequately prepared me. The only fish I caught that trip were between hatches, when obviously the fish were bored, careless, hungry, and had few alternatives. The next trip, Tricos were hatching, "at ten A.M.," they told me in the fly shop. And at ten A.M. they hatched, and I even caught a few fish. But that had been a decade earlier. The thought of tying tiny Tricos on now was intimidating, but hoppers? Vision-wise I felt young again.

The parking lot was empty. Things were looking better all the time. Then, despite my admonitions, Dan began wading down the middle of the small spring creek. I had learned the hard way that this approach did not work. The Slough requires stealth, but Dan, being Dan, had to learn the hard way too. Empiricism was what he called it; I called it a pain in the ass. While I sneaked around peeking through the weeds, Dan trudged along the same as he might have fished a freestone brook trout stream in Maine. But freestone streams gurgle, purl, and make many other well-chronicled poetic sounds that cover up the noise we make. Poindexter Slough is silent, glassy smooth, and clear. It is more like a bonefish flat than a brook trout stream. Except on the Slough, it is we who do the cruising.

I was about twenty yards ahead of Dan and had a front-row seat for the parade of panicky trout. I was reminded of the scene in *Jurassic Park* when T. Rex's approach is heralded by the visible vibrations in a glass of water. Trouble was, the fish spooked so far ahead of Dan that he couldn't see them, and he was skeptical of my reports. "Four fish just came blasting by at about forty miles an hour," I said.

"I didn't see them," he said.

"That doesn't mean they don't exist."

Fishing partnerships either survive this sort of thing or they don't. Ours had survived thirty years of it. (Later, he would have to tolerate an entire afternoon of my complaining about some dinky little stream in Idaho he thought was wonderful and I didn't, because I hadn't slept well and I didn't catch fish. He slept well *and* he caught fish. Where's the fairness in that?)

Dan continued trudging along, but now he was at least trying to trudge more stealthily. He was crouching and moving slowly. Nonetheless, plumes of silt flowed from each boot. "See any more fish?" he asked.

"Can't see much of anything now," I said. "Visibility is deteriorating rapidly."

Not long after that, he got out of the stream. I knew he would; he's not dumb. He's a man of science, and he just needed to see for himself that his way wouldn't work. Now he had, and now we could go fishing.

We moved off in different directions. The Slough curves and twists and folds back on itself such that it's possible to move directly away from one stretch of water and within a few yards hit more stream. After a while the terms "upstream" and "downstream" lose meaning. The willows and thickets along the banks hide the horizon (and that highway) and add to the sense of disorientation. After wandering around for a few hours, bouncing back and forth from one section to another, I had the strangest, most exhilarating feeling of being surrounded by trout. Caught some, too, half a dozen decent browns, no lunkers, but nice fish to fifteen inches, which, in that sliver of water, seemed large, and they were frantic fighters.

Their first move would always be into the vegetation; like rabbits diving into a briar patch, they'd plunge into the weeds. I lost some, but a hopper can accommodate a heavy leader, and I hoisted a few out of the grass into the light of day, where they seemed shocked, almost embarrassed that they, persnickety brown trout, had been fooled, and by such crude offerings as big hoppers with rubber legs, like bass flies! What was the world coming to?

Occasionally I'd encounter Dan, usually at the same spot. He had located a group of fish and was determined to make one take. He had already tried a number of different flies, different casting angles, but the easily visible fish defied him. He even invited me to try my luck (in Dan, a *real* sign of frustration). I declined. My fix on the situation was, if he had seen the fish for that long, they had seen him. Even though they hadn't fled, they wouldn't feed. My suggestion was, find new fish. He wasn't interested in my fix on the situation or my suggestion. Native New Englanders do not take advice from southerners on trout. In fact, he usually did outfish me, but that day he didn't.

When we met back at the parking lot and compared notes, it turned out that I had caught "half a dozen" to his "a couple." Sometimes it's best not to be too precise, and sometimes, the best times, we simply lose track. For me, this was just such a day. Numbers aside, I was much happier than he. I was euphoric; he was ready for a beer. On the same day, under identical conditions, we had entirely different fishing experiences. But it wasn't until the end of the week that I realized just how different our experiences had been.

We were heading to the airport, already reminiscing and rating the different waters we'd fished. We quickly agreed on number one. That was easy, and even though it is hardly remote—it is roadside—it shall remain unnamed. Second choice was where we split. Dan's second choice was that pissant stream in Idaho; mine was Poindexter Slough. Rather than accept that tastes differ, we tried to settle the issue by arguing. I won the argument; you'll have to take my word for it. I won it easily. I scored heavily and often. My best shot was "Well, maybe if you found yourself in Chilly, Idaho, with time on your hands, that little stream of yours *might* be worth fishing. Otherwise . . ." But you probably have to have seen Chilly to appreciate what a bon mot that really was.

In fairness, Dan landed a couple of good shots too, one that I still haven't fully recovered from. His main objection to Poindexter Slough was that the setting ruined the fishing experience. It was too close to town, too accessible, too civilized, too— of all things—urban.

Worst of all was I-15. He had a fixation on that highway. Those big trucks really bothered him. (What trucks?) "It's just not like fishing in Montana," he said. "It's more like fishing in Augusta, Maine."

I was stunned. I could not imagine two less similar places than Dillon, Montana, and Augusta, Maine. The geography, climate, culture, and, of course, the fishing were totally different. So what made him say it, other than to inflict pain, to pay me back for what I'd said about his second favorite stream? How could anyone not love the Slough?

I've given the matter a lot of thought over the ensuing months, and my conclusion is, he didn't like Poindexter Slough because the Slough didn't like him. The Slough did not respond to his rough ways, his ram-the-fly-down-the-throat approach, his stubborn efforts to pound that one pod of fish into submission. The Slough does not yield to force. Success with the Slough requires subterfuge and guile. Southerners may not know much about trout, but we wrote the book on subterfuge and guile. (Naturally, it's not called that.) The Slough rejected Dan's crude advances, and he resorted to name calling. Augusta, Maine, indeed!

I am convinced that if the Slough had favored him as she favored me, if he had caught what I caught, he would have *loved* the Slough same as I did. As always, the secret lies in the fish. That is their power: they alter our perceptions. They change not just how we feel, but what we see, and don't see. I saw a spring creek meandering through an idyllic green pasture, a Garden of Eden. Dan saw a big highway with a stingy little "crick" running under it.

His reaction and his comment made me wonder about my fishing experience in Augusta thirteen years earlier. Suppose that dark, sluggish salmon had been a fresh, bright fish, just in from the sea, its flanks still speckled with sea lice? Suppose it had tailwalked and somersaulted instead of wallowed? What if it had stripped line in furious, reel-burning bursts of speed? How would Augusta have looked to me then? Would the city have seemed like the quaint New England town it once was, and even now in some places still is? Would the handsome and historic Fort Western on the river's eastern shore have been more noticeable than Statler Tissue? Would the church bells have tolled louder in my ears than the traffic noises? Would the old buildings downtown have seemed quaint instead of just old? Would Augusta have glowed as luminously in my memory as Dillon, Montana, still does?

Too late to find out now. The Augusta dam has been removed. The fishing action has moved upriver to Waterville. What a dump that place is. I think.

Urban Guerrilla Angling

Seth Norman

Fishing in hell might look like fishing at Albany dump at midnight, those years when they filled-and-burned a long peninsula out into San Francisco Bay. Vents of smoke would hiss out from tangles of rebar and broken concrete while rats moved darkly, squabbling with each other and with the gulls for the rights to tear at cellophane wrappers and the rest of society's rind.

We wanted an outgoing tide. For that we'd risk the mile hike from the racecourse parking lot, long rods swinging and plugs rattling in a pouch as we picked our way farther out onto the peninsula of fill; that's when the anchovies would draw down off the mudflats, pulling back from gray shallows as humps of lost tires broke through like photos of Loch Ness. We could see the schools gathering, sometimes, in the scattering light from halogen lamps on the petro-pier across the cove. These images mingled with reflections of pier fence, meshed steel and coiled razor wire.

Then we'd hear them—not the baitfish, but hunting splashes of stripers in a channel offshore. The anchovy hordes ran a gauntlet

that hundreds of their thousands would not survive. Big as men,
the pounding bass sounded. Our signal.

Not an easy beat to wade, especially with the tidal wash dragging
at Red Ball waders patched solid to the knees. I remembered
dropoffs only as my front foot failed to find purchase—panicking,
then falling back because it was better to splash down into known
territory behind me. But wade we would, to make our casts
count, put the plugs out to where our prey waited for theirs.

Futile efforts, more nights than not. Stripers were already
dying out in the bay, millions of their young sucked into pumps of
Pacific Gas and Electric upstream in the delta. That was even
before Fish and Game warned us away from eating striper flesh,
tainted with heavy metal.

So then, never great fishing—one bass a night for two of us, if
we were lucky. If not, we still had slack tide in which to drift cut-
bait, maybe tentacles of squid on a slip-sinking rig. A leopard
shark or ray was inevitable; there were other possibilities. Twice I
was spooled here by fish I'll never identify—soupfin shark? sturgeon?—mysteries which left me gasping, actually frightened by a
speed and sense of enormity beyond any other I've felt through a
rod. Better than three hundred yards, took one of those fish, without ever slowing or turning his head.

Hellish, maybe, but ours alone. Mine alone, sometimes: those
years I worked P.M. shifts in a psychiatric hospital, leading a
restraint team. I clocked out at 11:15 and would arrive at the race
lot half an hour later. Often I'd still be riding my own tides, the
swell and ebb of adrenaline rush and caffeine shakes muted by
shots of cheap whiskey as I walked. Better to cast off my nerves at
the dump than bring them home to sleeping children. Better to
cast at the moon than lie beside their mother.

I left her about the same time as my last trip to the dump. A
fruitless quest: Well into a new day I took the trail back toward

my car. I heard men before I saw them limned against the sky. They carried rods, so I relaxed and then tensed again, startled when I recognized their dress as we met on a rise.

Gang "colors." Or the costumes of "wannabees," who are worse, having so much to prove. A thousand yards out onto the spit, bridge traffic coursing toward Treasure Island beyond, San Francisco lost in mist and no one within earshot of an explosion.

"Hey man, you catch somethin'? Whatch you catch?"

I stopped, waited, shook my head. There were three of them, laden with buckets and rods, surf stakes, paper bags. The middle-sized one had asked. "Nothing tonight," I answered.

"Nothin'? Whatch you mean *nothin'?* Whatch you fishin' for? What kinda bait?"

"Plugging for stripers."

"Yeah—lemme see that thing—no bait? We got bait—what we got, nigger?"

" 'Chovies," said the smaller one. "Squid."

"We got worms?"

The biggest one, silent until now, snorted and shook his head. "Shee-it, man, ain't got no *worms.*" Then to me, "You know how big fish gets out here? You know how big?"

"Pretty big."

"Uh-huh. . . . Man, I hook me a sturgeon out here 'bout like this." He put down his bucket to measure six feet between his hands. "You believe me?"

"I know they're there."

"Tha's right. Took me a *hour.* I get him up to those rocks. He come up and lay there, look at me with his *eye.* You know how they *eye* look? Little eye—mean fuckin' eye. He look at me an' I know. I *know.* So what I do?"

The big one looked to his quiet companions—they knew—then to me. "I shoot that mutha-fucker. Hell yes. I shoot him *again.* I shoot that mutha-fucker *seven times* wif a nine-millimeter.

You know what? He *don' die.* Mutha-fucker break off. Whatch you think 'bout that?"

I laughed. His companions glared at me, but the image of the sturgeon staring as this man shot him . . . so much for catch-and-release.

The big guy laughed also, after a moment. Long, loudly. "Tha's right," he said. "Tha's *right.* You believe me. See, niggers? He knows. So tonight, what I do, I come ready. Oh yes—I got fuckin' clips. I gonna shoot out that fucker's little eye, I am, tonight."

He shook his head, grinned. "Le's go, niggers. Hey, man. . . . Man? You have a nice night."

"Thanks. Good luck."

"Thanks. You too, you too."

I went to live with a cop who'd separated-to-divorce two weeks before. We fit his stripped bungalow well and, in one of those partnerships AA deplores, toasted our misled lives every evening. It was the absence of sleeping children that opened holes.

"Popeye," the other cops called him, not for the movie role, but because of his arms. He was just what you wanted in a peace officer, big enough to body-slam a bad guy, sane enough not to if given a choice.

"You fish, don't you?" he asked me one night. On the way to the lake he swore me to secrecy.

Inland, a short cast from a freeway, the lake had been part of his beat for a decade. People avoided the place after sunset because of the bodies found there. Killed elsewhere as a rule, Popeye insisted, by drug dealers and pimps; but he carried a .38 for the minutes we'd spend launching his raft. "Mostly it's just gay cruisers here at night. You'll see them by the boathouse unless it rains." See them we did, then and in the years that followed, men approaching each other in silence, moving away together into trees or to cars. AIDS was already endemic; these fellows seemed to me as insubstantial as shadows, wraiths. "A system," said Popeye. "They have signs. Used to be scarves and keys and whatever. Now, I don't know."

It wasn't these cruisers for which Popeye loaded the .38, however, but for those who hunted them. The gays were easy marks for robbers and worse. "Sport, that's what it is. Guys come out just to hurt them. That's weirder than what the gays do, if you ask me. Let 'em live, let 'em die; leave them alone. . . . Come on, let's catch fish."

And we would, though even Popeye had no idea about how the stripers first came into this place, or how long they had been there. All he knew was that every year they grew bigger and fewer and that a nine-inch, broken-back Rebel would take them.

Astonishing, how the world around us would fade on that little lake, contract to black water and low bank even as a thousand cars an hour rushed past, their lights and the city's mingling to obscure the stars. A perpetual plume of steam from a factory nearby looked soft and cloudlike, lazy; nighthawks, stoop-shouldered and solitary, stood guard on docks as we passed; migrant ducks in flocks—scores, sometimes—edged away from our approach, leaving webs of intersecting wakes.

Sanctuary. To the lap of water against inflated chambers and the hum of the motor, we'd talk of kids and cops, of the mad and criminal "clients" Popeye and I shared. It amused us that I had no tolerance for his "thugs" and that my "lunatics" gave him the willies.

Then we would lapse into silence, hands listening to the thrum of our lures along the rods.

Thissst—the line would hiss off the water as a striper came up—always the same way—to take a plug in its jaws, breach clear of the surface and crash down like a three-meter diver. The raft would jerk back or snap around—"Geezuz!"—fish from seven pounds to three times that, battles of ten minutes or twenty. "Feel this! Feel this one!" one of us would say, passing over the rod. "Can you believe it? Wait a minute—is that a buoy? Look out now—"

Releasing was difficult. A desperate striper of size will play havoc in a rubber raft, or even alongside, so we took to cutting back treble hooks to doubles, then to crushing the barbs . . . I remember trolling into dawn once, hunched up in wool like a warm worm, so quiet with exhaustion I was entirely happy.

I moved into a place of my own so Popeye could keep his kids on the weekends. We still met at the lake. Steve joined us, my fishing partner of a decade, then a cop friend of Popeye's. We'd plug from shore, take turns with the raft until Steve and I spent $50 on the shell of a small sailboat, refitted the teak, relaid fiberglass.

And sometimes I'd fish there alone. On a whim, almost, after the late news.

"Careful," cautioned Popeye.

"Why? Why do you do it?" asked a new girlfriend. I neither knew the answer nor felt a need to question myself.

"Is it a thrill thing? Because you know you can get hurt there."

True enough. On shore, this game was not safe. The moon saved me one night, illuminating a man stalking me tree-to-tree. Little valor in my discretion then.

I returned later, this time not so lucky.

A dock extended a deep-water drop-off where Popeye and I had hooked fish from his raft. Too close to the cruisers, too well lit and exposed, I chanced it anyway.

"I want a fuckin' beer!" shouted the man as his boots hit planks behind me. Not tall, hard to say how heavy in his coat. I turned and, with my left hand, dropped the rod down between us, to let hang there the gang-hooked plug.

"You hear me, cocksucker?"

In my right-hand jacket pocket the steel of protection felt reassuringly cold. It lent me calm as he came toward me walking fast.

Perhaps he'd taken me for a cruiser, timid and easy. Perhaps he'd already had a beer too many; I think the light served me better than him. In either case, he seemed not to notice the rod and lure until I gave a shake as he closed, hooks just a yard in front of his eyes. He stopped suddenly, confused, then determined again.

"I said—"

"The waitress won't be out for a while."

It's a nervous tic of mine, to make cracks like that. Fight, flight or quip. The habit disconcerts some; I could see him pause to inflate his frame. "Uh-huh . . . You think that's funny. I want money, funny guy." Then, as if the nature of his desire would be important to me, "For a beer."

That made him an amateur—no question now. If he was unarmed, then I never need thumb back the hammer. "Good luck," I said.

He stood silent for a moment while contemplating this stand-off. I saw his shoulders relax, then shrug. I kept the plug at level with his eyes.

Suddenly he laughed. And he was rueful when he spoke—"You're not going to give it to me, are you?"

I said nothing. He took a slow step back, another, then stopped. With a wide sweep of his arm he encompassed the lake, the freeway, the gay zone, even the plume of steam from the factory beyond. "Man, what the *hell* are you doing here?"

I don't remember that I said anything at all, but the question I'd ignored from others was oddly compelling from a bully-boy's mouth. "Taking what's mine," was the answer that rang in my head. Onto that I would embroider rationales and explanations, answers including my need to seek the feel of a striper coming up, the sound of waves and the sight of nighthawks hunched at attention. I needed these edges of earth and land, city jungle and untamed world, extremes of solitude and companionship, solace and excitement. I needed the taut hope of a cast.

Taking what's mine and risking a little, like the anchovies on the flats and a striper in the channel. Mine is the adventure, risk and pleasure as basic as hunger or the precarious urge of gay cruisers in the dark. Take nurture and nature where you find it. Sometimes there's release and sometimes it could end with seven slugs. I won't defend the wisdom, but at times I still gamble the night while my children sleep.

RIVERS IN EXILE

Paul Schullery

It was almost thirty years ago that I first found a life in Wyoming, working as a ranger-naturalist for the National Park Service. I discovered grizzly bears and trout streams and beckoning trails and the wild country that protected them. I was filled with passionate enthusiasms that have never faded and that I have sometimes written about just to help me understand why it all means so much to me.

Now that I live in the Rockies all the time, I suppose I've gotten a little complacent about its somehow being a life I'm entitled to. But when I started, it was something that I struggled to maintain and that I regularly had to surrender for extended stretches of time. Most often, those stretches involved periods of unemployment or graduate school, when I would return to my parents' place in a southern Ohio town of about forty thousand people (a "town" in Ohio, that is; it would be a city in Wyoming or Montana). Generous, good-humored, and endlessly patient, my parents put me up while I finished a quarter of school, or crammed for some required-skill examination, or just waited until

I could get back to Wyoming. The food, the housing, and the emotional support were all anyone could ever hope for, but I missed the wild country almost beyond endurance. A few times I escaped to fish Michigan's trout streams with my brother, but mostly I just moped along waiting for it to be over.

My restlessness drove me out on endless walks, and it didn't take me long to find my way to a small creek that trickled through a high-banked ditch along one edge of a small public park just a few blocks from my parents' house. Once I noticed it, I often went back, and began to count on it.

Water is always more or less wild. We pen it up behind dams, we run it through pipes, we spread it over fields, we slosh it around in bathtubs and swimming pools and teakettles, but water always obeys the same fundamental physical laws. Most of all, it obeys gravity. Even when appearing motionless, the water is responding to gravity—pushing against what contains it, piling up on what is beneath it, and always storing energy that can do all sorts of extraordinary things if it is ever released. And unlike living organisms, water does not have to exercise patience. It just sits there. But the instant it is free, it quite literally goes wild. No delay, no fanfare, just motion.

This little creek in my neighborhood was that way. Though imprisoned by high banks and cluttered with shopping carts, rubber sandals, hamburger wrappers, and less savory urban litter, it had no choice. And in late winter and early spring, when low flows left most of its ditch bed dry, the water expressed its loyalty to gravity in a wonderfully visible way. In a process whose actual details professional hydrologists apparently still argue over, the creek began to meander.

To my sight, the creek's path of least resistance might have been a straight shot down the middle of the flat bed of the ditch. To the creek, the bed of the ditch was not flat, but a microcosm of the broad lowland valleys of countless rivers on the planet, where the water responds to subtle contours, changes in soil density, and other influences, finally becoming the classic meandering river so celebrated in song, art, and the souls of anglers and other river addicts everywhere. Here in this little ditch, though I couldn't see them, were so many irregularities and inconsistencies in and under the soil that the creek was bound to deviate from a straight line. And once that process began—perhaps it only took the stream entering that stretch of straight ditch at an odd angle to set up the action—the creek became what wild water virtually always becomes, given the chance. It became a winding river, only a few feet wide but possessed of all the independence of motion its tiny bed could accommodate.

Of course, once it achieved that, it had me. Winding rivers, like roads stretching to remote horizons, are archetypal images that we respond to on deep and murky levels. They beckon us. They beg to be followed. They make the big promise, the one with no clarity but all the power in the world. Snowmelt running off a slope, car-wash water running down a driveway, rain in a street gutter—as soon as water gets rolling and starts its show, I just have to stop for a minute and watch.

Rivers typically meander at rates and dimensions that are roughly predictable. The "wavelength" of the meander, which one authority defines as "the straight-line distance across one complete S of the winding course," is typically about eleven times the size of the river's channel. This seems to hold true no matter what the size of the stream, and my extremely casual observations don't give me any reason to doubt it. Having eyeballed streams from the tiniest trickle fresh from a subalpine seep to huge lowland rivers, I'd have to say this sounds like an entirely plausible generalization. Certainly my town creek was up to something on about that scale, interrupted by the occasional bald tire or cinder block that, like some immense hard-rock obstruction in a free-running Montana trout stream, sent the creek careening off in a different direction and launching a whole new set of meanders.

What makes all this so wondrous and engaging is that though the general pattern of a stream's course is predictable, the individual variation is endless. I know what will happen; I just don't know what it will mean this time. Like listening to yet another performance of a familiar Bach piece, or tasting yet another interpretation of a hot fudge sundae, or further exploring any great relationship you may have with any person, place, or thing, each new encounter only enriches the acquaintance. There are always surprises.

It seems odd, but perhaps makes a kind of perverse sense, that it took a creek as abused and destitute as this one to help me realize why moving water is so magical. Stripped of all the easy thrills—ecological health, spectacular surroundings, charismatic fauna—this little creek had nothing left to show me but fundamentals. Without the usual distractions of biology and landscape, I could appreciate those fundamentals for all their glory.

Standing on the Main Street bridge, or walking along the banks, I somehow found great comfort in the little creek's attempted restoration of wildness, its irresistible loyalty to fluvial process. Without succumbing entirely to fantasy, I could look at this tiny flow of water and make some happily familiar equations. The inside bends of some of the better-established meanders—these would be long, arcing gravel bars on a western trout steam—were sprouting new grass and weeds, the equivalent of the willows and even cottonwoods I might expect on the bigger counterpart. Tiny cutbanks appeared along outer bends, again familiar except for scale. I could see the pool-and-riffle pattern of larger streams, the repeating, predictable pattern of shallow and deep water that is described as "vertical meanders," the streambed going up and down just as it moves from side to side. It was all there, and sometimes I involuntarily looked for the "good places," the ones that, if the creek were thirty feet wide instead of thirty inches, would hold fish. I found more comfort in this than I would have thought possible, and I didn't dare think about it too long or I'd get homesick.

Upstream from the Main Street bridge, past the aging Burger Chef and the Kroger's parking lot and on up behind the hospital, the creek emerged from its own little forest. This reach, though still safely contained in higher banks, had been allowed more flexibility. It had time to entrench its meanders into permanence and, with the help of the cover and heavier bankside vegetation, to get back into the business of harboring life. One day, in a relatively sheltered bend (one fairly free of Dairy Queen dishes and newspapers), my angling search unexpectedly locked me onto the familiar shapes of several small fish. I had no idea what species they were; some kind of minnow, I supposed. They were elongated, had some indistinct lateral striping, and reminded me vaguely of perch, which I was sure they were not. There was one larger one, perhaps ten inches long, and three or four little ones "attending" it. They all held and swayed in their little run, barely covered by the water. They never seemed to notice me, standing there a little ways back from the bank, looking at them like they were a twenty-dollar bill on the sidewalk.

I suspected that the big one was a female and the smaller ones were males interested in spawning. I wondered if they lived in some deeper stretch but came up into this shallow run to spawn. I developed scenarios for their lives, which somehow was more satisfying than going to the library and looking them up.

Most of all, I wondered over all the endless miles of unattended streams in this region where fish like these—so many species, some native and some not—went about their routines and rituals with even less regard for us than we have for them. Lacking the size and cachet and pretty spots and literary celebrations and red stripes and preferred feeding habits that attract sportsmen or any other constituency, these fish were entirely without human justification, and except when we felt obliged to wipe out their kind to make room for some species we could enjoy more easily, their generations slipped by with all the anonymity and ease of some goggle-faced creature bumbling around a geothermal vent six miles deep in the ocean. They barely existed in our minds, and yet the sight of them that day was a great relief to me.

It has been many years since I've done much exile time, but I have never forgotten those fish. I have often imagined them and all their sluggish-water kindred, quietly going about their evolutionary business in a million undistinguished little runs and pools—dodging beer cans and backhoes, succumbing to sudden washes of pollution, as when some redneck changes his oil upstream, recolonizing their benighted realms, and all the while sustaining just a faint trace of wildness in a hard-used place. That memory mostly serves to sustain the gratitude that I still feel toward them, and toward their little river, for helping me get along in exile. But I suspect it has also elevated my awareness of the beauty of wildness wherever it happens, whether or not it attracts fly fishers, nature lovers, and others of our ilk, who tend too often to seek the easy thrill of remote wildness and neglect the wildness close at hand.

On Urban Shores

Ian Frazier

My friend Tim and I used to hit golf balls into the water from the shoreline of lower Manhattan. Tim ordered the balls by the gross, used, from a golfing magazine; they had scuffs, smiles, spray-painted dots, and legends like "Tri-County Challenge—'80" and "Lost by Dan Trivino" and "Molub-Alloy The Metallic Lubricant" and "Maintenance Supply Co. Huntersville N.C." We told ourselves we were working on our drives. All we needed was a place open to the water; usually, we could find cracks in the asphalt or concrete big enough to fit a tee. We picked our targets. Once, I tried to land a ball on a mattress going out with the tide on the East River. I didn't succeed, but it would have been cool if I had. Once, I bounced a flat, hard drive off the stone base of the nearer tower of the Manhattan Bridge. A following shot struck the inside of an immense, upreaching I-beam, ricocheted to the opposite inside, then sped diagonally down into the water. Tim hit a beauty across a dredged inlet by a construction site at Battery Park City, the ball socking into a distant pile of sand and burying itself in a small landslide. One that he aimed at a passing container ship fell just short of the hull with a white exclamation point of a splash. My best shot came from a pier on the Lower East Side one winter morning with five inches of snow on the ground. Placing the ball on snow had a psychological effect on me, and I hit perfect drive after perfect drive. A cargo ship came along, well out in the channel. I took careful aim, kept my head down, and stroked one of those unstoppable balls that seem to rise like music, octave by octave—would it hit that glass housing near the bow? would they call the Coast Guard?—as the ship moved but not fast enough: ship and ball intersected, and a puff of snow came from a metal hatch cover amidships. Half a second later, we heard the impact's muffled clang. The name of the vessel was the *John B. Carroll.*

Just after dawn one day, we were hitting off an abandoned pier by Rutgers Slip, upstream from the Manhattan Bridge, when a little guy who had been sitting there on a folding metal chair came over and began to talk to us. Pointing to the water, he said, "See that? Those're anchovies. Like you put on pizza." Until then, I had never looked closely at the water of the East River—assuming the worst about it, I suppose—but now I observed that it was indeed full of silver-sided baitfish swirling and boiling like noodles in soup. The school was thick down as deep as you could see. The guy continued to talk about anchovies and other subjects as we continued to hit. He had a hand line with what looked like a piece of lime-green surgical tubing for a lure. When he left, he picked up from among some broken pallets a big striped bass he had caught. We had not noticed the fish before. He carried it off—to sell in Chinatown, he said—by a scrap of plastic packing rope strung through its mouth and gills.

Soon after that, we saw in the *Times* that the International Maritime Organization had issued a prohibition against ocean dumping of non-biodegradable plastics—a category that would include golf balls. To protect sea life, the ruling applied to all oceangoing vessels, and to cruise ships' profitable practice of selling golf balls for passengers to hit. We had suspected that what we were doing qualified as minor vandalism; now, thanks to the I.M.O., we were sure. So we stopped (there is now a net-enclosed driving range on one of the Hudson River piers we used to use), and I began to think more about the guy with the striped bass. I had read about stripers—the game fish that can grow to fifty or sixty pounds or more, the trophy species sought by thousands of oilskin-clad surf anglers, the voracious schooling fish that sometimes chase mullet and menhaden and tinker mackerel up onto the beach, the anadromous swimmer that lives most of its life in the ocean and spawns locally in the Hudson River—but I had never fished for them.

I began to scout up and down the shoreline in Manhattan on bright fall afternoons. At a rotted wooden pipe that had the appearance of a large barrel extending into the East River at Twentieth Street, I saw alewives nosing against moss-covered pilings. More bait appeared in the semi-clear water in sudden relief against the dark background of a drowned car seat. In fact, from Twenty-third Street all the way down to the tip of Corlears Hook, just south of Grand Street, the East River depths glinted with shifting schools of bait. All the books say that where there's bait there are stripers. I bought a nine-foot surf-casting rod and a spinning reel with twenty-pound-test line. I bought one-ounce white leadhead jigs with tails of white bucktail hair, and other lures. Stripers are known to move at dawn, to feed by first light. I woke up at four one morning and took the subway to Manhattan from my apartment, in Brooklyn—the first time I had ever approached a fish by going under it. "Striped bass," the token-booth clerk said when he saw my fishing rod. I rode with transit workers in orange-mesh vests carrying sacks of tokens and accompanied by armed guards, got off at the East Broadway stop, and walked down to the East River in the late night of Chinatown. A starling's raspy cry startled me. Police cars idled; clouds of steam from a steam tunnel crossed the street.

At the southern end of Corlears Hook Park is a graffiti-covered brick structure about the size of a shed, which extends into the river. The structure has no windows—only metal vents on two sides. Maybe it is part of an airshaft for an underwater tunnel. Warm air comes from the vents sometimes, and people who fish here call the structure the Heat House. A good cast from the Heat House's concrete apron can reach a tidal rip that forms on water ebbing around this corner of Manhattan Island. I set up my rod and tied on a lure by the light of a street light and went through a break in a chain-link fence. A man was sleeping on the concrete behind the Heat House, however, in the warm air from the vents. He had one shoe on, the other beneath his head. I moved to the walkway along the river upstream and began to fish there. The bottom of the river must be a cluttered spot—I hung up lure after lure. At first light, gulls began to fly by. I heard the rattle of shopping-cart wheels as a bottle-and-can-collecting guy appeared. The man behind the Heat House woke up and left, and I took his place. I was casting the bucktail jig about fifty yards to the tide rip, retrieving with short, quick pulls. Truck traffic on the Manhattan Bridge had slowed to a standstill, and on the bridge's lower level the bright beads of the D-train windows slid back and forth. Occasional passing barges sent wakes sloshing along the shore. The first jogger went by, singing tonelessly with his Walkman. At almost the moment of sunrise, about four minutes past seven, I felt a strong resistance on my line. I thought at first that I was hung up again. Then the resistance began to move. I pumped and reeled, gaining line. I still wasn't sure what I would pull out of there—an infant car seat, say, would have been only a mild surprise. But then the resistance was pulling, jerking. In the murky water I saw a flash of white, then stripes—a striper! It was about two feet long, and bent my rod double as I tried to hoist it out. Then there it was, slapping around on the concrete.

Striped bass are in many respects the perfect New York fish. They go well with the look of downtown. They are, for starters, pin-striped; the lines along their sides are black fading to light cobalt blue at the edges. The dime-size silver scales look newly minted, and there is an urban glint to the eye and a mobility to the wide predator jaw. If they could talk, they would talk fast. Although really big stripers take on a no-neck, thuggish, rectangular look, ones this size are classically proportioned—fish a child would draw. I unhooked mine and picked it up with both hands. All muscle, it writhed; a sharp spine of the dorsal fin went into my hand, and—thump, bump—the fish was back in the water and gone. A woman jogger doing leg-stretching exercises on the fence looked at me unsmiling, as if I were a fish abuser. Generally, when I fish I am in the woods, standing in weeds or mud or sand. Hauling a fish into the city like this made both city and fish more vivid—as if a striped bass had suddenly arrived flopping on my desk. A few casts later, I hooked another. It was about the same size but fought harder, and I had more trouble getting the hook out. Scales scraped off on the concrete as I held the fish down. I was too high up to reach the water, and so could not rinse the slime from my hands. I let the fish go; here a striper must be thirty-six inches long before you can keep it. (Also, because of the danger of contamination from PCBs and other chemicals, the State Department of Health recommends that people eat little or no fish caught in New York Harbor.) I broke down my rod and walked back to the subway and got home in time to take my daughter to school.

I wanted to catch more and bigger stripers. I got striper fever. I read outdoor columns about stripers in newspapers and picked up angling newsletters in tackle shops and called recorded fishing tapes at a dollar forty-five a minute and talked to closemouthed striper anglers. In a tackle store in Bay Ridge, several striper anglers trading stories dropped their voices and leaned toward one another as I approached. Striper anglers have big, gill-like necks, wear clothing in layers, and yawn ostentatiously in daylight. They are famous for their divorce rate; the striper is a night creature, and its pursuers must be, too. I fished for stripers all this fall. Mostly, I went to Sandy Hook, the expanse of barrier beach bent like a crooked arm from the Jersey shore at the southern approach to New York Harbor. Sandy Hook is visible from Brooklyn, and from Sandy Hook you could see the Verrazano Narrows Bridge, the World Trade towers, and the sunrise on the windows of apartment buildings in Brighton Beach. People have caught many big stripers at Sandy Hook; it is among the prime striper-fishing grounds on the East Coast.

I knew nothing about fishing in surf. At first, it feels funny to park in a beach parking lot (Sandy Hook's beaches are all part of a national recreation area), put on chest waders, rig up, walk to an ocean stretching thousands of miles to Spain, and cast. My first day, I fished along the beach for several miles, using a swimming plug bigger than many trout I've been happy to catch. Casting it was hard work. I didn't know for sure how far into the ocean I should wade. A big wave knocked me down onto one arm. I climbed back on the beach and saw a sign in the distance. I thought perhaps it warned of dangerous surf. I walked over to it. It said:

ATTENTION.
BEYOND THIS POINT
YOU MAY ENCOUNTER
NUDE SUNBATHERS

The wind was blowing hard, lifting sand in smoky wraiths and rattling it against pieces of plastic trash. A half-buried strip of photographic film flapped rapidly with an industrial sound; it had dug a sharp-edged trench beside itself. The temperature was about fifty degrees—not nude-sunbathing weather. As I continued, however, I passed a trim bronze naked guy accompanying a clothed female, then a trio of old guys strolling along in hats, sweatshirts, dark glasses, sneakers, knee socks, and no pants. One guy said hello. I said hello back.

Mostly, I fished in the hours just before and after dawn. Sandy Hook, maybe twelve air miles from my apartment, is about an hour and a quarter away by car. I drove across Staten Island and through Jersey in light traffic, listening to radio programs with few commercials, sometimes following into a toll booth the four-wheel-drive vehicle of another striper angler. The millions in their beds on a full-moon night in October may not know that the beaches nearby are lined with hundreds of striper anglers, mostly men but some women, looking seaward as if awaiting an invasion. Darkness makes them more solitary. Anglers rig up by their cars' overhead lights and walk to the beach thirty feet apart in silence. I passed many anglers in the dark but never exchanged a word. When you can't really see the ocean, you hear it and smell it more. On clear mornings, dawn came up full and sudden, like houselights in a theatre, and the sun followed along behind. Venus was bright on the horizon to the northeast at five A.M. On cloudy mornings, dawn was dull, with occasional surprises: a red sun would pop up on the horizon, chin itself on a low ceiling of gray, and disappear for good; or, though the horizon stayed dark, silvery light would glisten on the water, and from a break in the clouds, celestially high, beams from the sunrise would spill down.

Sometimes the waves were like high hedges. Sometimes the sea just sat there and swayed; then, all of a sudden, a breaker would *whump* and the foam would be up under my arms. I cast and reeled, cast and reeled. A moment came when I could see my lure in the air as I cast, and a later moment when I could make out its succinct splash. The birds woke. If the tide was going out, gulls by the thousand occupied the exposed sand. A gull picked up a clam, dropped it to break the shell, failed, and kept on trying. Flocks of little gray-and-white shorebirds—sanderlings?—

stayed right at the waves' edges. Long combers ran the birds back up the beach like the flat of a hand pushing crumbs. As waves rolled to the shore, they made white broken shells on the bottom hop up into them with a sort of vacuum-cleaner effect. Pieces of shells bounced from the waves' tops. I sometimes hooked a shell or a piece of clam but (at first) no fish of any kind. After full daylight, the anglers began to give up and came walking back to their cars. They wore yellow slickers, red-and-black checked hunting caps, camouflage coveralls, Penn State sweatshirts. At the ends of their lines dangled swimming plugs, popping plugs, rigged eels, sandworms, bloodworms, gobs of clams the size of baseballs. Some guys said the fish weren't here yet, or the mullet hadn't arrived to draw them, or the water was too murky or still too warm.

One morning, I brought peanut-butter-and-jelly sandwiches and bottled water, and stayed. By eight-thirty, along the whole expanse of beach I could see only one other angler. As I watched, his rod bent. I walked toward him and saw him land a big fish and let it go. When I got near, I began to cast. I had switched to the same leadhead jig that had worked in the East River; most of the white paint had been scraped off it by now. At once, I felt a hard, unmistakable hit, and the line went tight. Briefly, the fish took line, and, briefly, I hoped it would be big. The line was going right into the near-vertical side of a wave; at the base of a following wave I saw a swirl from the tail. I backed up the beach and slid the fish out of the foam and into a rivulet the ebbing tide had cut in the sand. It was a striper, good-sized but still not legal, hooked at the hinge of the jaw. I held it up and the other angler yelled, "Way to go!" I set it back in the surf.

At a tackle store in nearby Atlantic Highlands, amid sand spikes to hold rods on the beach, lead-loaded priests for clubbing fish, spiked cleats for climbing on jetties, bottles of fish scent to spray on lures, basins of wildly wriggling eels, and snapshots of stripers bigger than a six-year-old child, I talked to a veteran striper angler named Frank. He worked there and had caught some of the fish in the pictures. He gave me a number of tips, among them the fact that stripers love bad weather—the worse the weather, the more the stripers like it. As a result, one afternoon I fished in a storm that descended from the north, covering the city and its lights like a fire blanket. I had to adjust my hat to the tightest fit, and when the rain hit my eyes it hurt. Wind blew spray from the wave crests like dust behind a car, and it rolled pieces of foam along the sand, where they dwindled in a blink. Whitish brown foam covered the sea farther out than I could cast. Near some sunken rocks, I lost a lure, and accidentally put my next cast in the same spot. Reeling in fast to stay off the bottom, I felt a hard tug. The line started moving up the beach, I went with it, and the next thing I knew I had a striper on the sand at my feet. I hardly looked at it, in all the rain and spray: it was like something blown in by the storm, like a fish left in somebody's pants after a dousing in a cartoon. And, unfortunately, it was another "short," as the striper anglers call them. The bells of a buoy clanged and clanged. On the dim horizon, in the Ambrose Channel, a three-masted sailing ship in silhouette slowly headed for New York.

The striped bass never did show up in any numbers in the surf at Sandy Hook this fall, as near as I can tell. Striper anglers stood in the parking lots with their waders folded down around their middles and groused. Guys trudging back from the surf through the beach-plum bushes had similar expressions of frustration. A few talked about last year, or another year, and how the stripers were chasing bunkers in the wash at their feet, how the bluefish ate until the bait was coming out of their mouths, how some mornings every guy came home with a fish. This year, striper fishing was said to be good in the surf at Montauk, and in Staten Island Bay, and at Cape May, farther south in Jersey. But not, for some reason, here.

Striper season on the coast of New Jersey remains open all winter. The wind was blowing trash cans around on my street the last time I went out. On the Verrazano Bridge at four A.M., the car felt like a plane flying in turbulence. Street signs were shaking back and forth and flashing their reflections. As soon as I turned onto the road that runs along Sandy Hook, salt spray began to streak the windshield. I drove slowly down to Parking Area F, and as I got close my headlights picked out the waves lurching from the dark like shrouded beings in a horror movie. They were mobbing the beach: there was no beach—just waves breaking so fast as to have no rhythm at all. The wind was trying to shout them down. I walked to take a closer look, and a speedy long surge chased me back. I decided I wanted to be in the car. As I backed out, a comber broke over the sand barrier and came down into the parking lot. I turned up the car heater and headed for home. People say the stripers will return again in May.

THE CHUBS

Richard Chiappone

They are ugly little fish, the chubs. Four or five inches long, thick-bodied and snub-nosed, with dull eyes and rude white mouths. They are trash fish, junk fish, and their presence in a stream is a sign that something good has come to an end. But they were the only things in the sluggish little creeks around my town that would rise to my home-tied flies and clumsy self-taught casts, and for a time one spring I was a chub fisherman.

Mornings I drove my father to his job at Hooker Chemical, my textbooks on the seat between us, my rod in the trunk behind the spare tire. My father sat with his lunch pail on his lap, his hard hat between his feet. He ran his fingers up and down the spines of my books as he talked about the jobs for college students at the plant.

"Shipping," he said. "Try for shipping, or labeling. Those are the cleanest, the safest. They don't pay like production, but you're only going to be there summers. I mean, if you were coming into the plant for the long haul, God forbid, then you'd have to think seriously about the money. Capiche?"

"Labeling," I said. I was not really listening. We were in slow traffic on Buffalo Avenue. The morning sun slanted in between the factory walls, each beam of light flooded with graphite particles fluttering like a hatch of black insects. We had the windows down, and I could have closed my eyes and named the plants we passed: Carbide, reeking of rotten eggs—the sulfur dioxide that even a failure at chemistry could identify; International Graphite, smoking like a new tar roof; DuPont, its eye-watering solvents stinging the warm morning air.

We pulled up in front of Hooker, the always-leaking chlorine gas deceptively clean and bleachy smelling. The stack whistle went off with a window-rattling blast, and a flock of gray and black pigeons burst from their roosts in the pipe racks overhead. I watched them flap away around the smokestacks in a panicked curve, as if they'd never heard that whistle before, as if they hadn't spent every day of their pigeon lives right there on those shit-splattered nests.

My father glanced at his watch. "I wish I could get you into R and D. But the lab boys' kids get those jobs every time."

I said, "That's all right, Pop."

Something on the windshield had my eye. A small brown caddisfly was crawling along the wiper blade, its speckled wings folded tentlike over its back. A #12, I thought. Maybe a #14. I had both sizes in my fly box in the trunk.

"No, I mean it," my father said. "I wish I had more juice with personnel." He had the door open and was backing out. He snugged his hard hat down onto his head.

I looked at the caddis again on the windshield. Definitely a size 14. "I'm not set on anything." I shrugged.

My father shook his head. "Good Christ. You don't even know what to be afraid of."

I said, "I'm afraid I'm going to hear the story of how Bobby Dimiglio caught twelve thousand volts from the bus bars on the chlorine cell. The burns? The plastic nose they had to make for him? How he still hears buzzing every time he walks under a power line. I'm scared shitless I'm going to have to listen to that again."

He had to laugh. "College man. Smart." He picked up his lunch pail and turned to go, giving my books a little rap with his knuckles. "Anyhow," he said, "it was *thirteen* thousand volts, smart guy. Study hard."

"Sure, Pop," I said.

He wasn't aware that I hadn't been to a class in weeks, though exams were less than a month away. He hadn't seen the warning letter that had arrived with my dismal grades at the end of the fall semester.

I watched him through the chain-link fencing as he began to climb a steel staircase that took him up into a cloud of steam, and in a moment I could no longer see the stairs under his feet, only my father in his hard hat and coveralls, rising through the mist.

As I pulled out of the parking lot, the pigeons were already settling on the pipes overhead. I drove straight to Six-Mile Creek and the chubs.

Six-Mile may have had some natural beauty once. I don't know. By the time I discovered it that year, it had been trenched out and channeled around the new apartments and condos springing up along River Road. For most of its length, it was just a ditch, really. There were chubs in every part of it.

At the mouth, where it emptied into the Niagara River, I could see their dark cigar shapes filing past by the hundreds. Under the docks, where it had been dredged out for the boat basin, they cruised around the wooden pilings like cutouts on a spinning mobile.

I always fished upstream, away from the construction noise from the new subdivision. There was one natural bend left in the creek there where a stand of sumac and wild grape had been spared the bulldozer's blade. The bushes crowded the bank and were taller than a man, and standing among them, I couldn't see the apartments or the boat basin, just a wall of vines and new budding leaves and the creek swirling below it, high and cloudy with runoff from the parking lots and freshly planted lawns.

There in the thicket, I felt like I was on a real stream, and I cast to those chubs as though they were wild mountain trout. Sometimes I would catch and release them all day, the hours racing by until it was time to pick up my father at the plant. But there were also times when the chubs were as finicky as game fish, slurping the real moths and ants off the surface while refusing every imitation I offered. Then, when my best patterns drifted untouched, my mind would start to wander. I would begin to notice the sounds of the framing carpenters just beyond the bushes. I would begin to see the factory haze drifting over the big river and the rooftops of the apartments. And I would become keenly aware that a few miles away my chemistry class was just starting, or maybe calculus was ending, or that if I left at that second, I could still make ROTC that afternoon.

I would think about a girl in English 110. Her name was Wendy, and she wore army fatigues and had the straight blond hair and pouty lips all the girls from the radical dorm seemed to have been born with. I used to sit near her and plan our camping trips to the Rockies, Yellowstone, the Sierra. She would bask nude in the sun while I fished high-country streams for cutthroats and rainbows. Still nude, she would cook over a small fire, the smoke clinging to her skin and her hair for hours afterward. It should go without saying that we'd spend a lot of time in the sleeping bag.

I thought about our English instructor, Jeremy Stone, a graduate student and self-described "political anarchist." I wasn't sure what that meant but had a vague idea that bombs were involved; he looked capable of that, with his wild black curls and matching beard. He drove a Harley to school, wore leather pants and the same black turtleneck for weeks at a time, a sweater with a hole under one arm that winked open and closed like the white mouth of a chub as he gestured wildly before the class. He looked like a guy who hadn't fished a day in his life, and Wendy never took her eyes off him.

No one with any common sense or pride fished for chubs, of course, so I almost always had Six-Mile to myself, though one day as I was walking back to the car, I was surprised to find a man wearing a gray jumpsuit with a Chevy emblem across the back, sitting on a galvanized minnow bucket, still-fishing in the boat basin from a grassy bank opposite the docks. He was obviously a line worker from the GM plant up River Road, and sitting like that, in his uniform with his bait rod propped up in a forked stick at his feet, it looked like fishing was his job.

I don't know what he thought he was doing there with live bait. The only fish in the creek were the chubs, and they were hardly larger than minnows themselves. He may have heard something about pike running there. People were always starting such stories about some little ditch or pond or swamp in the county. There was never any truth to them. I think he was just killing time before punching in for the afternoon shift, because he stood and began reeling in just as I arrived. When he set down his rod and stooped to pick up his bait bucket, the gulls in the marina swooped down from every light pole and piling. They hovered above him, screaming and jockeying for position. He glanced up at them, took the lid off, and heaved the contents of the pail straight up into the air. The bait water geyser rose and hung there a second, the minnows glittering in the afternoon sun, the gulls, wild now, spinning into them in a blur of white feathers. Then the whole thing collapsed. The water and the bait and the birds crashed into the basin, and the air was empty again. The fisherman picked up his tackle and headed back to the parking lot.

After he had driven off, I went down to the bank where he'd been fishing. I set my rod in his forked stick and sat on the grass, watching a lone gull swimming in a tight circle in the middle of the basin, its head cocked to one side, convinced there was still something good to be found there. I noticed that I could look out the mouth of the creek and down the big river and see the Chevy plant, and I was appalled, and I swore that my life would never revolve in such a grubby little orbit, that my future would be different, special somehow. I think I believed that.

Each afternoon, when it was time to leave, I would take my rod down and hide it in the trunk, stash my fly box, wipe the creek mud from my shoes with a rag and put that in the trunk too. Then I'd pick up my father and tell him, yes, everything was going fine at school, and no, I hadn't had time to apply for the jobs at the plant. And that's the way it went for the last month of the semester and into exam week, though toward the end, my father quit talking about the summer jobs, and about school, and finally grew silent altogether.

On days when I had no classes and no car, I slept late and spent the afternoons tying flies, or just sitting on the porch listening to the radio. The Beatles were still big that year, the Byrds, the Yardbirds, the Kinks, and the Stones. My little brothers were in school, my mother working a few afternoons a week at the front desk at the Holiday Inn. I had the whole house to myself, the whole empty neighborhood, and it seemed that it would go on forever like that. And then suddenly the semester was ending, and I was seized with the feeling that I had to get busy and do something.

The night before my last scheduled exam I was sitting at my desk, studying the Herter's catalog with its ads for rod-building kits, fly-tying thread, hooks by the gross, when my father came into the room.

"You eat?" he said.

I told him I had eaten.

He sat against the edge of my desk next to a stack of outdoor magazines. He picked one up, thumbed through it. I watched him peer at the photos, reading each caption carefully. I realized that I had never seen him read anything but a newspaper, that he had no hobbies or interests I could name, that when he wasn't working he was doing chores around the house or yard, or helping my mother with the little kids. He closed the magazine and held it on his lap. He seemed to be thinking about what he had read, and I wondered what he'd found in there that puzzled him so. Then he leaned forward and pulled back the window shade a bit and looked out at the street.

"Pretty quiet," he said.

"There's nobody left."

I meant the guys my age: Jimmy Augustino and Cosmo Poretti had joined the army right out of school and were somewhere in Vietnam. Johnny Ruswicki was in disc jockey school in Minnesota and trying to convince the draft board it was real college. Keith Sweeney had died of an overdose, and Joe Spano was in prison for helping fix the needle in Keith's arm. The younger guys, our little brothers, didn't live out on the street the way we had. Where were the whiffle ball games? The home run derbies? These kids didn't seem to exert the kind of presence we had on the neighborhood. Maybe it was the TV. People were just beginning to blame it for everything. Maybe they were right. In the next room I could hear the hum of the set, my brothers laughing at Andy of Mayberry, or the Beverly Hillbillies.

My father let the window shade fall back into place.

"I take it you're not coming into the plant this summer."

I told him that the Rigi brothers were talking about painting houses. "I think they have some jobs lined up."

"Painting." He nodded. "I see." He stared at my unopened schoolbooks, but I couldn't read anything on his face except the exhaustion that was always there on work nights. Finally he said, "You're not coming into the plant because you're not going back to school in the fall. Am I right?"

"I don't know," I said. I was stunned that he knew how badly I was doing.

"And you don't much care for the army?"

He said that as though he just wanted to get the facts straight. Like he was taking notes on a curious life outside his own.

"I have some time. I'll go to Community in the fall, get the grades up, apply again for next spring." I heard myself saying that, and it sounded reasonable, but "fall" and "spring" were just words for things too far away to have any meaning.

"You understand I got no need for you to work at Hooker?" he said. "Maybe painting's a good thing for now. It's outside, at least."

It occurred to me that he was acting now, sparing me any further embarrassment. I didn't know whether to be grateful or furious.

"Sure," I said. "I'm going to be all right."

"Sure." He couldn't keep the sarcasm out of that, and I felt my face burn, but I held my tongue as he sat there quietly. After a while, he said, "Something happened at the plant today." He looked at me, but I waited. "An accident," he said. "Guy named Seekins. One of the rebs. From Alabama, I think. I didn't know him well."

"Chlorine?" I remembered the day we got the news about my father. My mother bundling us up and into a cab for the trip to the hospital. I remembered my father in the big white bed, with tubes in his nose. I was so afraid of those tubes, and angry with him too. How could he lie still and let them do that to him? I remembered the coughing fits he had for days afterward, the way he would gulp a glass of ginger ale and then burp a tremendous, booming burp that left the whole room smelling like bleach.

"No," he said. "He stepped off the loading dock and hit his head on the truck. Fell maybe three, four feet."

"Dead?" I knew the answer already.

"Yeah, dead," he said, and it sounded like it was my fault somehow. Maybe he was just angry I had made him say it. "Very, very dead," he said, quietly.

He stood to leave. He still had the magazine in one hand, and he flipped it open to the page he had marked with his thumb. There was a photo of one of the great sportsmen of the day, Lee Wulff maybe, or A. J. MacLane. The man was holding a huge Atlantic salmon, upside down, by the tail, smiling broadly into the camera. My father held it up for me to see.

"Fishing," he said. "Grown men? I don't get it."

I almost started to say something, but it was clear he was not about to sit still for any lecture on the merits of fishing. Not from me. Not just then.

"I'm just saying, I don't get it," he said. He set the magazine down and walked out of my room.

I sat at my desk for some time, listening to the sounds of the house shutting down: my father wishing my mother good night as he turned in first, my brothers going off to their room when their show ended. A little later my mother knocked lightly on my door, three soft raps that were her way of saying good night without disturbing my studies. Then the house was quiet.

I wished my mother had come in. I wished she had come in and said something. I wished my father had said something more, something definite or demanding that would have made clear to me what I should do next. But the house was silent.

After a while, I went to the kitchen, dark but for the small bulb in the range hood that threw a weak glow across the kitchen counters. My father would be the first one up in the morning, and my mother had his thermos standing ready by the electric coffeepot. On the kitchen table, my brother's school project, a salt and flour map of New York State, looked like a deformed pizza. I stared at the lumpy Adirondacks and Catskill mountain ranges; Lake Champlain, painted in bright blue poster paint. Beautiful places in my own state I had never seen. I took the car keys from the hook by the door and went out.

I drove to Pine Bowl. Bowling was out of favor with guys my age, but besides the alleys, Pine Bowl had a sizable billiards room. In the middle of the night, that's where I could always find one or two friends who had managed so far to avoid both the army and steady work.

The drinking age was eighteen then, and I ordered a beer and turned to find an old friend, Frank Machek, standing at the bar next to me. Frank used to live in the neighborhood when we were in grade school. We played down at the river at the end of the street, spearing carp in the warm green water near the sewage pipes, stoning the wharf rats, building trash fires. We'd take willow sticks and retrieve the rubbers that floated in the backwaters and boat slips like strange white eels. We called them Tonawanda whitefish, and burned them in our fires, along with all kinds of flotsam: snarls of fishing line, bits and pieces of Styrofoam, plastic bottles and jugs. Frank taught me to do "pickle-on-a-platter" when the girls came down where we were skinny dipping. He showed me how to burn the leeches off my ankles with an eight-penny nail heated to glowing in the fire. I thought we'd be friends forever.

Then, in eighth grade, he moved to another part of town, another school, and I lost track of him. Now he was wearing his hair down over his ears and had grown a sickly Fu Manchu mustache, and I kept studying him to find the old Frank I'd grown up with. He said he'd spent the last year traveling to Mexico "on business." I steered the talk to fishing, and he told me about trout streams in Colorado and New Mexico where the water was so clear the fish seemed to be suspended in air, and then I could see

him again as I'd known him, with his flattop and his waterlogged
Keds. We had a few beers and he revealed that he was on proba-
tion for a pot bust, and that he would not be leaving town again
soon. So I told him about the chubs, how easy they were to catch.
I asked him to join me.

"No can do," he said. "I start at Bell tomorrow." He winked.
"Look good for the court."

I tried to imagine Frank working an eight-hour shift at the
huge aerospace plant on the edge of town. I tried to imagine anybody my age doing that.

I said, "Frank, they're going to give you a two-inch brush and
a pot of glue, and you'll be sticking canvas to chopper blades till
your back cracks. What kind of life is that?"

"A life," Frank said. He laughed. "A fucking life? I'm supposed to listen to that from a guy who fishes for chubs?" He
walked off, shaking his head.

I finished my beer and tried to sort it all out, because I have
always been one to try to sort things out after a few beers—
though it never comes to much. Frank Machek on the assembly
line, Cosmo and Jimmy in Asia, Keith in his grave, and Joe in
prison, the death of that guy Seekins at Hooker, a man I'd never
even met. What did any of it have to do with me?

I walked out of Pine Bowl into a dense, black fog. One of the
graphite plants was pulling a night discharge, something they did
(then denied) all the time. In the swirling carbon dust, the big
parking lot lights looked liked twenty-watt bulbs. The moon was
lost in the black sky. A layer of fine soot covered my father's car. I
ran the wipers and the windshield washers all the way home,
hunched over the wheel and squinting through the smudged glass.

_____

The next morning my father acted as though I were dropping
him off at work and going to school as usual, as if he believed I

was really planning to take my exam. We didn't talk much, and when we did, we confined it to the haze hanging over the city. It was late May, hot and humid, and the black carbon dust stuck to everything. It clogged my nostrils and built up in the corners of my eyes. People were sweeping their sidewalks, hosing down their driveways. The little Italian man who owned the motel across from Great Lakes Carbon was out by the swimming pool trying to skim the black film off the surface with a push broom.

When I pulled into the parking lot at Hooker, my father didn't make a move for the door handle. He looked up at the factory looming before us: the tall wire fences and brick walls, the crisscrossed maze of rusted steel beams, the steam lines and gas lines and power lines snaking through the plant like tangled arteries and veins—everything leaking and dripping and crusted. For a long moment he sat and stared at it as if he'd expected to find something different there that morning. Then he turned to me.

"Let's go," he said.

"Go?"

He nodded. "You've got the light." He pointed to the traffic signal, and waved me forward with one hand. I pulled back out onto Buffalo Avenue, mystified.

"Where are we going?"

"You pick. I'm with you." He leaned back into the seat, put his feet up on his hard hat.

I said, "Pop, come on. Really. What about your job?"

"Stop at the Texaco. I'll call in."

"You're taking the day off?" I felt the hairs on my arms standing up.

He shrugged. "I need a break."

"What are you going to do?"

"Let's do whatever you do all day. You know, a typical day, say."

The big vein in my neck began to pound. "A typical day?"

"Now you got it."

The entrance to the Thruway was approaching on the right. I put the turn signal on. "Typical?"

"Typical," my father said, and I turned onto the ramp and toward Six-Mile Creek.

That far from the factories, the sky was still blue. Although technically it was spring, it was warm and the summery odor of outboard gas was in the air. There were a dozen boats moored in the marina: cabin cruisers and smaller skiffs. An oily rainbow shimmered on the surface of the water around the docks. In the middle of the boat basin, a huge flock of bright white gulls bobbed in a raft.

"This is it?" my father said. His look seemed to say he had expected a little more.

"I guess so." I put my rod together and headed for the creek, wondering when he was going to put an end to this. But he just fell in behind me, and there was nothing I could do then but keep going.

The air was alive with mosquitoes, midges, and gnats as we walked along to my place in the sumac thicket. Brown and yellow grasshoppers catapulted from weed stems before us. I watched the chubs rising in the shallows, their fat gray bodies spiraling up to the surface like little missiles. My father made his way beside me, taking in everything but saying nothing. When we got to my spot, he took a seat on a tussock of new grass, folded his arms, and waited. And so I fished.

The chubs were feeding like never before, and they hit nearly every cast, no matter where it fell. Sometimes two, even three, fish would streak toward the fly. If one spit the hook, another would devour it before I could retrieve. At times they struck while it was still in the air, inches above the surface.

I poured myself into it, forgetting the summer ahead and whatever came after that in the fall, forgetting my father behind me sitting in his coveralls and work boots watching me move up and down the bank taking chubs from behind every rock and midstream obstruction. I caught six in six casts behind a sunken lawn mower, three in a row out of the middle of a tire. I had never done anything so well in my life, and it was exhilarating. But after an hour or so, the weight of his eyes on my back was too much for me, and I reeled in.

"We need to talk," I said.

My father said, "Keep fishing. They're really biting, aren't they? What are they, bass? Some kind of bass?"

I studied him to see if he was joking, but he was not. "No," I said. "Not bass. Listen, Dad—"

He waved me off. "Go on," he said. "I'll tell you when to stop." He shooed me back toward the creek with the backs of both hands.

I looked at him for a minute, and then I went back to fishing.

I fished right through that day, not even pausing to eat, although my father went back to the car around noon and brought his lunch pail down and sat munching his sandwiches behind me as I continued to cast. I didn't know how long he intended to pursue this, but with or without food, I would last as long as he did, and I was ready to keep on until dark, or maybe until the creek dried up that summer, or until it froze again the following fall if I had to.

But when the action started to slow sometime in the late afternoon, and the fly floated a dozen drifts without a rise, I knew it was over, and I turned away from the water, about to admit that I had had enough, ready to move on to whatever came next between him and me. I found my father lying on his side in the sunny grass, resting his head on one arm and snoring softly. I walked up and stood over him. His face looked gray and dry next to the moist new grass, the skin on his hands cracked and red. He had shaved that morning, but his cheeks were sharp with gray stubble again now, and he looked so terribly old that I turned away, feeling I'd looked upon something I was not supposed to have seen.

When I looked back, a small blue moth had landed on the rim of my father's ear. It was a startling, chalky blue—not only its powdery wings, but its body, its legs, and its head. Even its twitching antennae were fine blue feathers. I found myself staring at the rhythmic flexing of its wings. While I watched, another identical moth landed within an inch of the first. An instant later a third and fourth joined them, and others clustered in the air around my father's head. I looked up to see that hundreds, maybe thousands, were now fluttering around us and just above the creek, their fierce blueness almost iridescent against the cracked mud banks.

Upstream and down, the moths continued to arrive, hard to see at first against the sky, then suddenly visible as they dropped low and hovered in a fluttering cloud inches above the water. In minutes the creek was covered with them and seemed to run as blue as the rivers of my dreams. I thought the chubs would materialize and tear into them, but nothing broke the surface, and the moths slowly began to lift off untouched. I watched them rise, not scattering across the fields the way they had come, but hanging together now like a flat blue ribbon that streamed upward and over the bushes and then the rooftops of the apartments, and finally disappeared into the blueness of the sky. I was still looking up at the empty air when my father awoke.

He squinted up at me. "You done?"

"I think so," I said. "I think I am."

He sat up and looked at the creek for a moment. "OK, then," he said. "Give me a hand up."

We walked back down to the car in silence again. Clouds were banking up over Canada just across the river, and when a shadow passed over us, I was hit with a wave of late-afternoon sadness I would know again and again throughout my life. I loaded my stuff into the trunk and looked up to find my father peering toward the city so intently I had to look that way too. Even after he had turned away and gotten into the car, I remained staring.

From that distance I could make out the tops of the smokestacks and cooling towers over the factories, and high above them the remains of the graphite cloud, just a thin layer of black then hovering over the plants as though someone had taken a pencil and drawn a line across the sky to separate the pure summer blue from everything that lay below it.

But what I could not see was myself there among them ten years down the road, with a wife and children and none of the skills needed to support us. What I couldn't see were the layoffs and cutbacks and plant closings, the lines at the unemployment office stretching down Pine Avenue and around the corner, the past-due bills, the loans unpaid, the credit cards full and the checkbook empty. What I couldn't see was the journey back and forth across the continent in search of work, and a marriage collapsing as love gave way to shame and blame and the sure death of affection that goes with that whole life. What I couldn't see was me going to my father with my hand out like a beggar, like a stranger in need.

It was all out there in front of me, but as I got into the car, all I saw were the chubs rising again in the boat basin, their mouths blossoming like white flowers.

Looking back now, after all this time, it's hard to believe that that's all there was to it, that my father and I didn't talk about anything of importance on the way home from the creek, didn't discuss what I had done, or was going to do. Or not do. And if my failures disappointed him or hurt him, he didn't let on. I waited for days, for weeks. I waited for years. But he never mentioned it again, and I took his silence to mean that my life was mine to do with as I pleased. And so that's what I did.

What else was I to think? I was young, and I was a fisherman.

ÎLE DE LA CITÉ AND PARIS FISHING

James Prosek

"Papa, papa!" said little Marlin looking up toward his father.

"No, we cannot bring the fishing rods," said Pierre. He hoisted Marlin onto his shoulders, and we walked under the drizzle to Pont Neuf and down to the Place du Vert Galant over wet cobbles to the tip Île de la Cité.

"There are two islands in the river here in Paris," Pierre explained, "Île St. Louis and Île de la Cité. These are the two best places to fish. When the river is in flood, the fish stack up in the eddy downstream of the island where the current is broken. There are probably five hundred bream here. They especially don't like current, and at times the big *silure* come to feed on them. You would not believe, but you will see! They open their giant mouths and eat a four-pound bream whole. While you were skiing, my friends Jean-Pierre and Guy hooked eight off Île St. Louis. They landed one that was about thirty kilos and lost one they said would have been nearly fifty—that's over 110 pounds!"

West of where we stood was the metal bridge, the Passrail des Arts, on the left bank the Musée d'Orsay, on the right the Louvre.

Downstream were Île St. Louis and Notre Dame Cathedral, whose bells then indicated it was well into the afternoon.

"This is the most beautiful pool in the world," Pierre said, passing Marlin to me as he climbed over a rail, "and the fishing gets better every year. The Seine was very polluted in the sixties and the only fish that lived here, if any, were carp and eel. Now there are thirty-eight species in downtown Paris. I only started catching silure two years ago, small ones. This is the first year we have caught such monsters."

"And you eat them?" I asked Pierre.

Pierre looked at me through his glasses, raising his gnomish nose and scratching his wavy hair. "Oh yes, we eat them," he smiled as if to assure me that I would eat them too. "The Seine is clean; my friend André insists that in a year or two he will swim in it. The source of the river in Burgundy is a spring-fed trout stream. We will fish it in May and we hope to find a nice hatch of mayfly. Both François and Vincent have access to excellent trout fishing on the haute Seine."

"Did salmon ever run up the Seine?"

"Yes, of course, all the rivers draining to the Atlantic in France had salmon. The run in the Seine was magnificent. The last one caught in Paris was in 1956." Pierre stopped to carry Marlin up the steps to Pont Neuf again by the statue of Henry IV. "Well, who knows," he continued, "maybe we will get one tomorrow morning. Maybe Guy and Jean-Pierre can join us. We'll fish until about nine in the morning, and then we must go and set up for the fly-fishing exhibition."

That night, I slept wrapped in a wool blanket on the floor of Pierre's office. At eight he knocked on the door, came in with his key, and woke me. "Well, we slept too late," he said standing over me, "but that's okay, I think. We have a long day ahead." He looked at his watch. "Let's walk down to Île St. Louis anyway, to see if Guy and Jean-Pierre caught anything. We'll leave the rods behind this morning."

Guy and Jean-Pierre lived in a poor neighborhood in the out-skirts of the city. A chef in a school cafeteria and a landscape worker in a cemetery, they supplemented their meager incomes by fishing most every weekday morning before work and selling their catches to local restaurants. As far as Pierre knew, they were the only commercial fishermen in Paris, and illegal ones at that. Their most coveted catch was the zander, or as Americans call it, walleye, a sweet, white-fleshed fish. Guy and Jean-Pierre could earn up to a third of their normal monthly incomes through their fishing.

Pierre and I walked along the Seine on the Quai des Orfevres to the facade of a newly renovated Notre Dame Cathedral, dim and ominous in the morning light. "They are wonderful fisher-men, these guys," Pierre told me of Guy and Jean-Pierre. "I met them four years ago fishing on Île de la Cité. One of them had caught a ten-kilo zander. I couldn't believe it! So I started to follow them and fish with them and made a small film of their fishing. I gave Guy a cell phone to call me if they caught a big fish, and I would ride my bicycle down to the river with my cam-era. I got them sponsorships through American fishing tackle manufacturers, so they now have good free equipment. They mostly fish with worms and they are very skilled. It takes a great deal of skill to fish a worm correctly—as much as it does to fish a wet fly."

At this hour of the morning, Paris was quiet and the city belonged to the fishermen. The river was a beautiful eggshell brown and made the limestone facades of the city buildings seem a more luminous yellow and the zinc roofs a deeper gray. "They're out there, see?" Pierre said as we crossed Pont St. Louis to the Île. The fishermen were two dark shapes on the tip of the island, standing with their lines in the water.

" 'Jour, Pierre," one said as we approached them. They had caught a bream and killed it. It lay bloodied on the cobbles. I shook each of their hands.

"Well," said Pierre, looking into the opaque water, "if the bream are here the silure should be too." We stayed and watched them for a half an hour, but neither Guy nor Jean-Pierre had caught a fish, so we left to go set up booths at the fly-fishing exhibition.

The Salon de la Peche à la Mouche was an annual fly-fishing exposition at the Espace Auteuil, near the Bois de Bologne in west Paris. Represented there were a hundred or more vendors from Austria, Belgium, France, Holland, and Iceland, selling everything from flies and fly rods, wine and swine, to antique salmon spears and trips to exotic destinations.

Pierre was certainly the prince of the show—everyone seemed to know him. He filmed and aired a weekly fishing program on French television and edited a fishing magazine called *Pêches Sportives*. When we got to the space, Carole, his wife, was setting up a booth with some of Pierre's antique tackle and fishing books. I was to help Pierre set up a kind of museum-style exhibit he'd prepared on the history of salmon fishing in France. During the course of the day, we drove several van loads of wares across town from Rue Dauphine to the Espace Auteuil, including some sculptures by Pierre's friend François, which would be for sale in a small art gallery space.

As a consequence of our work, I met François Calmejane for the first time, the tax-inspector artist who had created the big iron sculptures of flies that hung in Pierre's apartment. He looked a bit like an inspector, with a bowler-type hat, a thick black mustache, and a Sherlock Holmes-style pipe with a deep curve in it. He was wearing a bright-yellow shirt and a tie made of wool, and over that a vest of green ostrich leather. The hair on his head was a kinky dark brown. He held the pipe between his yellowed teeth as he spoke gently and affirmatively. "Just one moment François," Pierre said, seeing him try to lift a heavy sculpture by himself. "We're almost done; we can help move some things."

"François, you know," Pierre told me in confidence, "is one of the top tax agents in France. He's busted a lot of big guys who were doing corrupt things. He takes four weeks of vacation every year; two of them he spends with his wife camping and fishing for trout in Ireland, the other two he spends making his art."

I imagined the inspector up in the small attic space above his apartment that was his *atelier,* creating the visionary sculptures in a two-week orgasmic gesture from ideas and energies stored up for an entire year. At that time I didn't really have a sense of who François was. Though he seemed a little cold, I could say that I had never seen anything like these sculptures he had made. Clearly he had an obsession with fish, and when I had the opportunity to see his studio, I felt I would be walking into his mind, which would be strange but also familiar as I thought I might see a bit of myself in there.

The sculptures themselves, besides being sublime and terrifying, were dangerous to carry, as they had all kinds of sharp objects protruding from them—scythe blades, giant hooks, spears, knives, and chains. You had the sense that if you fell on one, you'd be impaled and bleed to death.

All of the sculptures of flies and fish were imaginative and brilliant, but one in particular was, to my mind, a masterpiece. Pierre thought so, too, and said so when we had set it up and were standing beside it.

"This one I think is his best work. It really is remarkable. François calls it *Le grand bécard vainqueur!,* 'the great male salmon that won.' The head," Pierre said, pointing, "is the actual head of a salmon that I caught in the Baltic and brought back for François, and the fishing reels in its stomach are mine too."

The sculpture depicted a large salmon with its tail touching its head as if it were leaping in triumph. Its body was a series of curved wires creating a cavity that could be seen into like a cage. Its tail was a fishing rod handle and an explosion of various lures hung on spiraling lathe chips. Its pectoral fins were large gaffing hooks. Its air bladder was a gas tank from an old French motorcycle, its intestine was a scythe blade, and in its gut were various items of a fisherman's kit—reels of different shapes and colors, lures, flies, and a landing net. They symbolized a salmon that had overcome all the obstacles it faced on its journey up the river from the ocean; it had swallowed all the anglers' tackle, broken their lines, and cursed the industry of man.

Pierre and I were on Île St. Louis the next morning with our lines in the water. Pierre fished with a worm and gave me a heavy rod rigged with a big lure for silure.

"I think Jean-Pierre and Guy are fishing at Neuilly," he said. He picked up his cell phone to call Guy to get a report.

"What? Yes, Guy? Two bream, no silure. Okay. What? *Vraiment? Okay, à tout à l'heure.*" Pierre put the phone in his pocket, laughing and shaking his head.

"Did they catch anything?"

"They caught two bream and Jean-Pierre hooked an ear."

"An ear?" I asked, thinking I'd heard wrong.

"Yes, apparently," Pierre said, casting.

"You mean a human ear?"

"That's what he said," Pierre said, casting.

"What did they do with it? Are they going to tell anybody?"

"What, and cause trouble? They are just fishermen."

After an hour of fishing we'd caught nothing so we left to be at the exhibition early—it was the first morning that it was open to the public.

Pierre spent the morning trying to sell exotic bird skins to Dutch fly-tiers who used the feathers to make salmon flies. "We don't need parrots and blue chatterers," one said.

"How about these bustard feathers?" Pierre said.

"They are no good to us without the matching feather from the opposite wing."

"Five hundred francs for all of them then."

"You are asking too much, Pierre," one said. "Your birds are not in very good shape." They turned the birds and folded the skins to expose the feathers and show how sparse they were. "I would take all of the skins for a thousand francs and even that I think is a lot."

"One thousand francs?" Pierre said, tucking his chin in close to his neck and lifting his shoulders, trying to sound insulted. "They're worth more than that, and I have much more bustard at home that I would throw in."

François, in the meantime, was standing amid his art, wearing his green ostrich leather vest, his pipe between his teeth, and a glass of white wine in his hand. He stood beside the only other artist selling art there, a beautiful woman named Marie-Annick who did lovely pastels of fish.

"Did you catch anything this morning, James?" François asked me.

"No, not a bite."

"I love fishing in the Seine, but only in the summer. I never catch fish with Pierre this time of year."

Fishermen walked by the art, mounted on stands and hanging on the walls, but only François's friends stopped to look for very long. "They're not interested in art," said Marie-Annick. François poured her a glass of wine.

"It's true," said François opening another bottle. "They're only interested in the latest technology in rods and reels. They've lost their purpose; they've become too removed from real fishing. I love fly fishing, but they should try bait once in a while. It's more tactile." He took out a pouch, stuffed his pipe, and looked vacantly at the room, pretending that he hadn't just made a philosophical statement or was even capable of making one.

I left François and Marie-Annick briefly to look at a sculpture he had done of a big silure. Staring at its mouth, which was wide enough to accommodate a dinner platter, I began to enact the ritual in my mind of catching one, as prehistoric man once made drawings of the hunt and his prey on the walls of caves the day before leaving to kill.

"The fishing should be good tomorrow," Pierre said, stopping by to share a glass of wine. "It's raining right now. The river must be rising, and the strong current will force the bream to move into the eddy." He drank his wine. "The big silure will follow. When the bream are in thick, there are so many you can't bring a lure through the water without snagging one. The silure get in a frenzy. They herd the bream and sometimes push them to the surface, where they stun them with their giant tails and eat them." Pierre saw in my excited glance that his enthusiasm had been successfully contagious. "We'll fish every morning until we get one."

The next morning, I walked to Île St. Louis alone to go fishing, and passed only two people on the way picking up garbage in front of Notre Dame. Pierre came on his bicycle an hour later. The bells on the cathedral echoed off the river.

I was leaning against a black lamppost when I felt a tug on my lure—all I reeled in, though, was my lure with silvery fish scales stuck to the hook. "The bream are in," I heard Pierre say to himself, "the silure should be too." But they did not come to my lure that morning.

"Tomorrow we will get serious," he said.

At the expo that day, the final day of the show, I was consumed by François's sculpture of the salmon, *le grand bécard vainqueur*. It assured its viewer that the fish was a worthy adversary.

After eating lunch, Pierre and I walked in the rain to a fish market to buy mackerel and squid for silure bait.

"When I decide to do something, I do it seriously," Pierre said.

That night we prepared all the gear—six rods, hooks and weights, folding chairs, an umbrella, and wading boots—and stowed it in Pierre's van.

"Don't you want to refrigerate that?" I asked him as he loaded the mackerel and squid into a canvas bag.

"No," he said, "I want it to stink."

By seven the next morning we were on Île St. Louis. By seven-thirty all six lines were rigged and set in the water.

At that hour in February it was still dark. The lampposts were lit and the city was quiet. A light drizzle fell on my face as I lay down on a marble bench and closed my eyes. After a few minutes I lifted my head to see if Pierre was still there. I looked around, and in my half-awake, half-asleep state, the current of the river going by the island gave the illusion that I was aboard a moving ship. I also had the sensation that the ship was sinking, because the river was almost visibly rising from seven days of on and off rain.

Near sunrise, Pierre picked up one of the rods and jigged for zander. On the second cast, he retrieved the lure with a fish scale—slightly oblong, with a mother-of-pearl brilliance—stuck on the hook. "Bream!" he exclaimed prophetically. "It's a good sign for silure."

At this pronouncement, I stared at the lines with new hope, which lasted for about five minutes. My eyes were averted to traffic on the Expressway Pompidou—the morning migration of Parisians to the west side of the city.

When there was enough light to read by, Pierre pulled out a day-old copy of *Le Monde*. He read for two minutes, and then looked up at the lines. "Shit!" he said. "Where are the silure? We have done everything right here, and the conditions are perfect. If the rain keeps up they will have to close the expressway. Look, it'll be just a couple feet before it's underwater!" He walked over to our bait supply and, chopping several mackerel in pieces, started chumming the eddy. "Well, at least we are not stuck in traffic," he said, his bloodied hands throwing chunks of fish into the river.

"Shi-it, where are the silure?"

Several minutes passed.

Pierre laughed as he looked toward the right bank. "There is one now." He pointed to a long barge, on the cabin of which was printed in block letters, *Le Silure*. It was one of two sanitation barges for the city of Paris that clean the dog feces off the quays and scoop up floating debris, named after the bottom-feeding omnivore we were in pursuit of.

As the morning grew brighter, joggers ran by us around the tip of the island. People walked by with their dogs on leashes. The dogs sniffed our bait and tangled their feet in our lines. Shortly, the sanitation barge moored to the island by a large metal ring. A man in a green suit jumped out and began to hose down the cobbles. The bells at Notre Dame and other nearby churches sounded nine-thirty.

The Fine Art of Hudson River Fence Fishing

Nick Lyons

Fly casting on the new-mown grass in Riverside Park, I was pleased to see a fellow brother of the angle walk briskly through the crowd of skeptical onlookers. He had an army carry-all slung on his shoulder and a long and heavy saltwater rod in his hand; his nose was bright red and there was a pint bottle stashed neatly in the back pocket of his baggy gabardines. *Stenonema fuscum* had appeared on the Schoharie, my scouts had reported, but I had only caught a half dozen good clumps of fresh-cut grass in an hour of serious casting. They were about five or six inches apiece, I suppose, and I had slipped them off the unbarbed and, in fact, untipped yellow fly easily. They gave no appreciable fight.

"You never ketch 'em here," the angler advised, with a loud laugh.

"Where're *you* going?"

"The river." He came over and shook his head at my bamboo fly rod.

"What do you get?" I asked.

"Fish," he said. "What you get with toot-pick?"

"Grass," I replied.

He waved his hand down, laughed loudly again, and then, somewhat surreptitiously I thought, marched quickly off. I had seen that particular step before. It was somewhat too determined and hurried. A telltale phenomenon. The man had information that he was keeping from his brothers. Was there a striper run on? Could shad be in the river and available to the initiate? Herring?

My four children were with me and we had an intolerably long June afternoon, hot and landlocked in the city, stretched in front of us.

Why not, I thought: I'll try the river.

I sent Paul back for his spinning rod and Charles to the fish market on Broadway for twenty-five cents' worth of squid. Pier fishing, if that's what it was to be, was not new to me. When I was a kid I'd bike down to Sheepshead Bay or Steeplechase pier and fish for porgies, ling, whiting, blowfish, hackleheads, and whatever else could be scared up from the bottom. Most of them had scared me—with their horns and prickles, their ignoble inflating and deflating. It was a weird business, practiced in snow and boiling sun, and I had not regretted relinquishing it when I fell in love with trout—which at least had no horns and only grew fat in one's imagination. I had never tried the Hudson, though we lived only a block away, in the center of Manhattan. A slide presentation by Bob Boyle at the Theodore Gordon Flyfishers' dinner in March had intrigued me with the fecundity of the river, and I had, years before, caught stripers and even herring on flies as far north as Barrytown.

Without disjointing my fly rod, I took my two young ones by the hands and headed for the river. Twenty minutes later the spinning rod and squid arrived, and I was ready for action.

It was an exquisite day.

The sun was bright, the sky was pleasantly flecked with soft white-gray clumps of clouds. The New Jersey palisades were firm, angular, and green. A couple of posh cabin cruisers headed upriver; a long brown barge headed down. Several women were sunbathing against the slope of the hill; they had hardly any clothes on; one of them was more angular and firm than the palisades. A helicopter fluttered up the mighty Hudson like a bloated swallow—but found no mayflies rising.

I saw at once that this was not pier but *fence* fishing. There were some eighteen or twenty anglers spread along a hundred yards of fence. Their heavy saltwater rods were leaned at precisely the same angle against the railing, and all of them were standing back ten to twenty feet, alone or in little groups. There was one spirited group of eight to ten Puerto Ricans whose lively chatter rose above their loud radio music.

I found an unoccupied few yards, laid my fly rod carefully against the fence, set up the spinning rod, cut and threaded on a slab of squid, and cast out. I have never been the sort to leave a rod unattended—neither on the forked sticks common to reservoir fishing nor on piers—so I held it lightly couched in my arm, with my right index finger pressing against the monofilament. I even gave the line a few sporadic tugs, to impart some action.

After an hour, my older boys grew bored and went off to play baseball; Jennifer and Anthony ran to investigate the boat basin a couple of hundred yards downriver. I had experienced my share of family disasters while trying to fish for trout, and was enormously grateful that they could thus occupy themselves. I had perhaps discovered an anglers' paradise in the midst of gray New York. There were escape facilities for the children, music (if that's what you wanted), company, a beautiful landscape across the river, shapely sunbathers; there was no wasted time getting to the fishing grounds; there would be no anxiety lest the day's hatch be missed, or go unmatched. If it wasn't the Schoharie when the Hendricksons were on, and you were alone with fish feeding in every run and pocket, it was still—I rationalized—a line in the water.

But I soon discovered that Hudson River fence fishing is an art not to be taken lightly—an art with its own traditions and lore, its own ethics and mores; it is also essentially a traditionalist's art, for I'll wager there have been few changes over the past seventy years—nor any tolerance or encouragement paid the rebel. Innovation, as for the fabled lotus-eaters on the Beaverkill, is met with distrust bordering on disgust.

At precisely 3:27, one of the Puerto Rican anglers let out a momentous howl, not unlike that of the hound of the Baskervilles. He raced down the slope, grasped his rod, and struck it back five feet. *"Grande, grande!"* he shouted, and was soon surrounded by seven or eight onlookers. He reeled his line in without hesitation, with a sweep of his arm heaved his fish directly out, and a moment later there was a long green eel flapping and squiggling on the grass.

An interesting tool was then produced, which I had never seen used before. It looked to me like a piece of twisted wire hanger. It was carefully placed just ahead of the hook, with eel hanging down. Then, with an abrupt movement, the eel was flipped in a circle around the tool. Whatever was supposed to happen did not. The maneuver was nevertheless tried again and this time the eel came quickly and miraculously off the hook and flopped to the ground. There it was ceremoniously kicked at and stabbed with a long knife until it lay motionless. A mutt was brought near, but it showed singular disinterest in the long corpse.

Then a general query was raised whether anyone wanted the remains. There was no response and the eel was thereafter handled meanly by several children—until it disappeared.

I asked one of the men the name of the instrument used to disgorge the hook so handily. "Wire," he replied.

Soon another cry went up and another young man raced to his rod. Within the next twenty minutes another and then another rod were struck back fiercely, and four more eels were swiftly brought to fence. The rise was going full blast and, frankly, I felt somewhat left out. I reeled in my strip of squid and discovered it to be singularly unmolested. Anthony had returned and I asked him to seek out a good angler willing to part with a few worms—for that, I had now substantiated, was what they were rising (or sinking) to; I gave him a quarter and made him swear not to spend it for ice cream. He acquired four night crawlers (though bloodworms are considered slightly superior), and I promptly threaded a whole one onto my #10 Eagle Claw hook.

I continued to hold my rod and in a few minutes was rewarded with a few faint but telltale taps.

I must have been overanxious, this being my first eel, for I struck quickly and came up with a shredded worm.

My second strike came at 4:27. I gave this one more time, but again came up with only a mutilated worm and a long strip of tissue paper.

Several other eels had meanwhile been caught, and also one striped bass. My field notes concerning the striper read as follows:

Striper caught at 4:20. Bait: worm. Size: about seven inches. Fight: negligible. Miscellaneous comments: Angler claimed: "Got one about the same size, same time, day before yesterday." May be significant. Fish stashed quickly in bottom of metal box.

Soon after I missed my second strike, I realized that much more careful thought was necessary if I were to master this art. Careful observation is indispensable to the serious angler, and I soon noted the following: no other angler was holding his rod. In fact, there seemed a deliberate attempt not even to notice it. The fishermen would stand in a crowd, and then, either by instinct born of long experience, by sight, or from the tinkling sound of one of the small bells attached to the tip of many a rod, they would leap to the fence for action. The Hudson River fence strike is sudden and abrupt, delivered with killing force; I presume this is to compensate for the bend the river must put in the line, though it may simply be the natural hostility of urbanites.

There seems to be the widest latitude concerning the proper clothing for this kind of fishing. Short pants, Havana shirts (not tucked in), or no shirts, and leather moccasins appeared to prevail, though I observed four or five anglers in traditional street clothes. I could come to no conclusion concerning the logic for dress, and must assume my subsequent failures were in no way related to what I wore—khaki trousers, an Orvis vest, and my slouch stream hat.

I queried several fishermen who had displayed conspicuous success. Their characteristic mode of expression was laconic, authoritative, unequivocal. The following conversation transpired:

"Ever use plugs?" I asked.

"Nope."

"Spoons?"

"Nope."

"Any kind of artificial lure?"

"Nope."

"Why not?"

"No good."

"Have you tried them?"

"Waste of time."

I had noticed that one fisherman spit on the bit of worm he affixed to his hook, and asked him: "Why do you do that?"

"It helps."

"Ever catch anything on top?"

"Nope."

The angler I'd met in the park made me his confidant. He was extremely knowledgeable and perhaps felt some sympathy for me because I seemed to try so hard, I had four children who were by now embarrassed at my ineptness, because anyone who used toot-picks was in need of counsel, and perhaps because he had been the instrument of my conversion. Taking me under his wing, he promptly advised that I would never catch a thing if I persisted in holding the rod.

"You ketch 'em in the country like that, maybe; not here. See these places?" He pointed to some old notches in the railing; I had not seen them before. "You put rod there."

I was tempted to ask him precisely why, in order to learn whether these long green ropes were so tender-lipped that they could sense the presence of a fisherman, but he was intent upon imparting a great deal of information to me quickly, in order to get back to his bottle of Old Grand-dad, so I let him go on. I was not at all sure such an opportunity would present itself again. If he were indeed a deputy of the Castle, a secretary of the curia, I would not be caught napping.

"Your weight no good; you need three, maybe four ounces." I was using about a half ounce of split shot, pinched on and strung along a foot of line. It seemed to hold the bottom, and the spinning rod could not manage anything heavier. I told him so.

"You never ketch 'em," he told me flatly.

Spiritually, I could not quite work my way around to the four ounces.

"Your bait wrong," he said. "You need him little piece of worm, like this." He squashed off about a half inch of worm and was about to put it on my hook. Before I could tell him that I had always, in my salad days when I fished worms, done better with a whole bait, he added: "No. No. Hook wrong, too. You need long hook. I get you one."

This was downright decent of him, but I thought I could get them just as well on a short-shank hook and told him so. He shook his head and was about to give me up when I asked him: "Tell me the truth. Why don't any of you guys hold the rod?"

"No good."

"Don't you *like* to feel the fish biting?"

He roared with laughter and took my rod. "You hold this," he said, giving it to me.

I took the rod back.

"Now put finger on line." He gave the line at the end a few small twitches and then broke up laughing. I had to agree that this element of the sport had little enough to recommend it.

Since I had seen my friend keep several eels, I asked him if he ate them.

"Sure," he said.

"Even from the Hudson?"

I might as well have cursed his mother. He said nothing.

"Well, how do you cook them?"

He came over close to me and whispered: "You put nail in his head, then strip skin off, cut him in chunks and fry or stew him.

"Easy as that?"

"You stew him like beef stew." He made several facial expressions indicating gastronomical happiness.

When he left me, I condescended to put a bit of worm on my wrong hook and cast it out. Then I went back to the grass and lay down on the slope, closing my eyes against the warm redness of the sun, listening to the pleasantly rhythmic chatter, and thinking back a month to a May afternoon when the Hendricksons were popping up out of a still pool in the Catskills and riding slowly downriver like little sailboats until they were sucked under, dramatically, by the trout. A sparsely tied Red Quill, with genuine blue dun hackle, had done some happy business for me.

I was on my third trout when I heard Jennifer shout: "Our ball's in the water, Dad." They had been playing nearby. I got up slowly and went over to the fence. A tennis ball was bobbing slowly along the rim of the rocks. It belonged to the son of one of the regulars.

There was some immediate interest in this, and four or five of the more agile anglers hopped the fence and vied for the honor of fishing the ball out. One of them got way out on a rock and with a long stick proceeded to prod at the ball. It only bobbed under and farther out.

"What are those?" Jennifer asked, leaning far over the railing and pointing.

I looked. "Balloons."

"Oh."

The young man with the stick was now holding onto his companion's arm with one hand and leaning still farther out.

"Look," said Jennifer. "More balloons."

There were two more. "There must be a party upriver," I told her.

"Can we go?" asked Anthony.

"Look, he's got the ball," I said.

The young man had indeed dropped his stick and grasped the ball, but as he did so his foot slipped against the slippery rocks and he careened over into the river. Rather than alarm, this caused numerous shouts and cheers and considerable excitement. The man went under once, losing his baseball cap, splashed and shouted with animation—as one might, say, if he had fallen into a sewer—and then got a hand on the rocks, forced himself up by sheer will, and was finally lifted out.

There was mucho celebration.

But then it was noticed that his hat was gone.

Several men reeled in their lines and tried to probe for it with the rods, but only managed to push it farther out. Finally it got some twenty feet out into the river, with only a bit of the peak showing.

One good turn deserved another, so I reeled in my line, took off the half inch of worm, pushed the split shot down flush with the hook, and made several short underhand casts. I could not hook the cap.

Then I saw the fly rod.

While the hat was ever so slowly moving farther away, I clipped off my yellow practice fly and tied on a #8 Eagle Claw hook. Then, stripping line off my reel, and to the utter amazement of all the onlookers, I began to false cast. They watched in silence as the white line sailed back and then forward.

On the third cast, I was able to lay my line over the hat, and then, drawing it slowly in by hand was lucky enough to catch the hook onto some part of it. Alternately filling with water and losing water through the air holes in the top, and hooked but lightly, the cap rode in majestically across the majestic waters of the Hudson. It took some care and strategy to bring it to the rocks and then up and over the fence. At its best weight, the cap went a full two pounds, I guess, and gave a good account of itself.

The landing was watched with muted silence, and then, when the hat was safely landed, the event was greeted with what I took to be somewhat extravagant praise. I was toasted, congratulated, invited to share in the community bottle, and offered a long, thin, green rope, which had once been an eel.

It was late now, and I took my toot-pick and headed hand in hand with my young ones up the hill. A cool breeze had come on, and the near-naked ladies had long since left; the globed sun was cherry red and serrated with soft Payne's gray clouds. I could smell the new-mown grass and listened to the sweet methodical hum of cars on the West Side Highway.

At home a patient fishing widow waited, one who, like me, had never reckoned with the special delights of Hudson River fence fishing. Fortunately, I doubt if I can ever master this art. But it is well to remember that there's more than one way to skin a cat—or an eel.

HOW TO GET THERE: All major airlines fly to Kennedy, Newark, and LaGuardia airports. All regular train and bus lines come directly to New York City. The #5 Riverside Drive bus stops on the corner of West Eighty-third Street. Crosstown buses at Eighty-sixth and Seventy-ninth. Seventh Avenue subway. Do not come by car—parking not available.

BEST TIME: Same catches reported all year long. Come when you can.

ACCOMMODATIONS: Great latitude—from Waldorf-Astoria to nearby furnished rooms. Rat traps a necessity if you choose the latter.

COSTS: Will vary greatly; generally astronomical.

CONTACTS: Ask for Joe at the Eighty-fourth Street fence.

WHAT TO TAKE: Bring cheapest and heaviest saltwater tackle; four- and five-ounce sinkers; #8 long-shank hooks; a couple of night crawlers or bloodworms will last a day; all clothing acceptable. Transistor radios useful.

ADDITIONAL INFORMATION: Literature on Hudson River fence fishing is currently unavailable. No books on subject now in print, though it is probable dozens will be written in the coming years.

FISHING THE JAM

Jerry Dennis

My father never learned the art of snagging salmon. I realize now that is to his credit, but when I was seventeen and suffering from a serious case of blood lust, it was a matter of some embarrassment. My friends and I had become aficionados of the unadorned treble hook and I had little patience for a man who hardly tried. He stayed home that fall and fished alone for walleyes in Long Lake. I joined the crowd at the Boardman River in Traverse City and learned a hard lesson.

The river had filled suddenly and unexpectedly with so many coho salmon, a new and exotic species in our part of the world, that everywhere we looked we saw enormous fish porpoising, swirling, leaping clear of the water to land in great side-smacking explosions. It was hardly possible to drag a lure through the water without hooking one. My friends and I, drunk with abundance, figured we could be forgiven if we killed a few more than our share, or if we forgot—temporarily, temporarily—such concepts as restraint and honor and sportsmanship.

It was the beginning of our last year of high school and we were eager to be released to the broad freedoms of adulthood. Every afternoon, the moment the final bell rang, we ran for the parking lot and drove Doug's rust-shot Torino straight to the river. There, at least, we were equals to anyone. On the water we had already graduated to a bigger world.

We recognized many of the cars parked beside the bridge. Other students had skipped school, had been here all day, and would have raked the Willow Hole clean by noon. Below the bridge, the hardcore regulars, the Men, stood in ranks along shore. They crowded each other, their thickets of rods in constant up-and-down motion. They used surf-casting outfits with thirty-pound-test line and cast their heavily weighted lures like they were heaving anvils into the river.

We hurried into our waders, grabbed our spinning rods, and raced down a trail almost nobody else used, beneath tag alders and blackberry brambles, over piles of crumbling yellow bricks and tangles of the discarded monofilament line that stretched in coils and snarls from Union Street Dam to the mouth of the river. We busted out onto the riverbank. The pool was deserted. Fishermen were upstream and down—we could hear a wailing drag, the crash of a leaping salmon, shouts and curses and laughter—but somehow, this spot, *the* spot, had been left to us.

Doug, careless with knots and other trivial matters, was rigged first. Before he could cast, a large salmon broke the water at midstream; another swirled close to the bank. Doug tossed his Spider out and across, allowed it to sink the necessary three-count, then began the old jerk-and-haul.

"You bozos better hurry," he said. "Unless you want to watch me catch all the—Whoa!"

He was into one already. It ran downstream, his rod skewed low and rigid, the reel shrieking, the line tearing across the river so fast it raised a trail of mist on the water. Suddenly the fish came up: somersaulting in its own spray, arching and flexing, crashing back into the river. It was hooked in the back. Good spot. It gave the fish leverage but did not disable it with pain.

We had forgotten the net. Russ and I refused to go back to the car. Doug screamed at us to go but we ignored him.

I cast my Spider and let it sink. One-thousand-one, one-thousand-two, one-thousand-three. Wait any less and the hook would be pulled over the tops of the salmon. Wait any longer and it would get wedged in rocks, driven into a log, or tangled permanently in the monster-snarls of line that had been growing like fungus on the bottom since the run began. Yank and reel, sidearm to keep the hook low. Yank and reel. No resistance to speak of, just the #2 treble and the quarter-ounce bell sinker streaking through the water. Yank and Whoa! It ran instantly, the rod maxing out, the fish up and leaping before I could warn Doug to watch his line. He hadn't landed his ten-pounder yet, and mine, twelve pounds at least, crossed his line and his crossed mine and mine crossed his again. Then the two salmon plowed off in opposite directions and the lines broke almost simultaneously, like rapid-fire gunshots.

Doug blamed me, of course. He had a scrub brush of hair growing straight up from his forehead, like he'd been shocked. When he was angry he would push his glasses up on his nose; they'd slide down and he would push them up again. Russ, meanwhile, cast into the pool and on the first yank was into a fresh-run eight-pounder that blasted out of the water almost the instant the hook bit. Doug, to cool off, left for the car to get the net. I landed Russ's fish for him, waiting until he led it into shallow water and then placing my foot beneath its belly and booting it up on the bank. When Doug returned with the net, Russ had his fish hung on the stringer in the shallows, and I was into another, a coho that might have gone to ten pounds except that it was hooked in the absolute maximum leverage point of the tail and I didn't have a chance. It made a V-wake for Lake Michigan and kept going even after my line popped fifty yards downstream, where the fast water began at the Front Street Bridge.

The newspapers called it Coho Fever. It appeared shortly after the salmon began congregating near the mouth of the Platte River in northwest lower Michigan in 1967, eighteen months after they had been planted by the Michigan Department of Natural Resources in an effort to revitalize a Great Lakes fishery that was suffering, to say the least. Once considered sport-fishing heaven, the Great Lakes had become a wasteland. Parasitic sea lampreys had wiped out the lake trout, and massive schools of alewives— small, shadlike baitfish that had the unpleasant habit of dying by the millions every summer and fouling the beaches—were nearly all that thrived in the lakes.

Nobody knew if the salmon would feed on the alewives, or even if they would survive in the big lake. But when adult fish appeared in Platte Bay late that summer all expectations were surpassed. They had grown an astonishing eight to fifteen pounds in less than two years, and were returning to their parent stream in numbers that even the most optimistic fisheries biologists had not dreamed of. The fever became an epidemic. Mile-long lines of vehicles waited to use the ramps giving access to the lake, and frenzied anglers launched their boats the way a dump truck unloads a full bed of refuse: backing up fast to the ramp and hitting the brakes. They then would park in the loose sand along the road, getting their vehicles stuck and abandoning them there. Later, when salmon moved up the rivers, the fever moved up with them. I caught a bad dose of it.

We were not prepared for the salmon. Our equipment was inadequate and we had no idea what techniques might catch the fish. A few people were looking to the Pacific Northwest and Alaska for precedent, and a very few were convinced that the salmon could be caught in the rivers on conventional tackle, but most anglers believed that once a salmon entered a river it would show no interest in lures or bait. It was thought that since the fish would inevitably die after spawning, we were justified in harvesting them with any method that worked. That attitude was endorsed by the Department of Natural Resources, and snagging was legalized on virtually every Michigan river those first few years. It became the standard tactic of most river fishermen.

In the Boardman, in Traverse City, hundreds of salmon were stacked in every pool from the mouth of the river to the Union Street Dam, a distance of about a mile. Snaggers would fill their five-fish limit, carry the salmon home in the trunks of their cars, then return to fill another limit. Catches of twenty fish a day were not unusual at first, before the competition got intense. By then it was as entertaining to watch the action as it was to participate in it. Fishermen unequipped for the strength of the salmon watched their reels explode and their rods shatter. Full-grown men leaped into the river to do battle hand-over-hand with salmon that had smashed their equipment. Fishermen standing elbow-to-elbow at the hot spots became involved in incredible tangles of line when hooked fish ran parallel to shore. Harsh words were exchanged. Fights broke out.

My friends and I learned fast. We used sturdy fiberglass spinning rods and reels with smooth drags. Many of the snaggers preferred twenty- and even thirty-pound-test line, but we chose to use eight-pound-test, willing to lose a few fish in exchange for the greater casting accuracy of the lighter line. Refining our techniques, we became proud young masters of snagging. We devised our own snagging lure—the Silver Spider—a treble hook with a heavy bell sinker attached underneath by a few twists of copper wire. It was a deadly, streamlined weapon that rode through the water hooks upright, ready to impale anything in its way.

Doug, Russ, and I hooked six fish in six casts. We had never seen the pool so full of salmon. But our activity attracted the attention of fishermen above and below us and they were closing in. Russ made a hurried cast and lofted his Spider over a willow branch. Doug, laughing, cast sidearm to put his hook beneath the same branch, hauled back once, and nailed a big, silver female that did a tail-walking routine the length of the pool. Seven for seven.

I made a cast, jerked, reeled up, jerked, and was into another fish. Eight for eight. After hundreds of pounds of snagged salmon I knew immediately not only the size of the fish but approximately where it was hooked: head, side, belly, or tail. This was a small one, maybe three pounds, hooked amidships. I wasted no time, simply derricked it in and dragged it onto the beach.

But it was not a salmon. It was a brown trout, vivid with spawning colors, with the hooked jaw and thick body of a healthy, mature adult—the largest and most beautiful trout I had ever hooked. I had snagged dozens of salmon and never felt the slightest remorse, treating them like throwaways, like objects of commerce given out to promote business. But this was different. This was a wild, natural fish, here for a purpose that had nothing to do with the circus atmosphere of the mock run of salmon. I had seen other trout snagged. A few steelhead had entered the river, and they were sometimes snagged, netted, and hurried to car trunks by men and boys who laughed about their indiscretion. Possessing snagged trout was unlawful, of course, but the law seemed to be held in abeyance those days.

I was determined to release the trout. I kneeled and removed the hook carefully. The wound seemed shallow, harmless.

"What you got there?"

I looked up, expecting a conservation officer. He was a man, perhaps forty years old, dressed in street clothes and wearing aviator's sunglasses. Not a conservation officer. Not a fisherman, either.

"Brown trout. I hooked him accidentally."

"Accidentally. Sure."

"I'm going to let him go."

"Why let him go? I'll take him."

I had noticed people like him lingering on the fringes. They were not fishermen, but they liked to watch. Sometimes they cadged a salmon or two from the fishermen whose freezers were already filled.

"I have to let him go."

"Seems like a shame. A waste."

"He was hooked lightly. He'll be okay."

I noticed his trousers were too long and the cuffs had frayed where they dragged on the ground. He wore black, heavy-heeled leather shoes caked with mud. I looked up and he was smiling at me. He never quit smiling.

"It's just going to die anyway," he said.

"No it's not," I insisted. I was growing uneasy. I wanted to release the trout and see it swim away as if nothing had happened.

The man shrugged, smiling, and stepped forward. He raised his foot and brought it down heel first on the trout's head, crushing it into the gravel. The body jumped once, then was still.

Sliding his hand under the gill plate, he lifted the fish. "See?" he said. "It's just gonna die anyway."

I did not know it yet, but I was finished as a snagger. I would go home that evening not sure about what had happened, knowing only that the fun had gone out of it. In a few years the Department of Natural Resources would virtually abolish snagging anyway, limiting it to a few short stretches of the larger rivers, and eventually it would be banned altogether. Anglers, forced to experiment, would discover that salmon in rivers could be caught after all on lures, bait, and flies.

Standing beside the river, watching the man walk off with the mutilated trout, I realized my enjoyment had been tainted all along. We had caught fish, many fish, but it had been an empty exercise. Intent on having fun, we had failed to consider fair play. It was obscenely easy to convert abundance into waste, but at some point—and now it seemed inevitable—there must always be a reckoning.

HERMAPHRODITES TO DRIES

Dave Hughes

My wife, Masako Tani, is a well-known fly-fishing writer from Tokyo. Though we live in Oregon and call the brawling, sparsely populated, and largely unpolluted Deschutes River our home stream, we find it helpful to our happiness to spend a few weeks each winter visiting her family in Japan.

Masako's family lives in the Akasaka district of downtown Tokyo. When we visit, that's where we live as well, in a tiny building surrounded by others, some smaller, some taller. Tokyo is such a jumble of buildings, laid out on streets so few of which go straight for more than a few hundred feet, that the view from anything less than a skyscraper extends no more than the faces of a few buildings in any direction. If you grew up, as I did, not in a town of ten thousand, but five miles into the countryside outside such a tiny town, then the view from almost any spot in Tokyo is claustrophobic. You can't see far. You can't see trees. You never see fields.

Once or twice a visit, Masako and our daughter and I take an expensive tea-and-crumpets snack in one of the restaurants atop a forty- or fifty-story hotel, at an uncrowded hour, just so I can get a view with some distance to it. Even up there, though, the view, including distance as it does, reveals only buildings. I look around at the cities within the city, clusters of tall buildings poking up out of the flat landscape of five- to ten-story buildings, and see a Seattle here, a Portland there, a Boston on the skyline. I have not found a place in Tokyo from which I can see beyond the borders of that broad, confining city.

I get up early each day during our visits to Japan and write undisturbed until noon. After lunch I bundle up our daughter and head out on a round of nearby parks. That gives Masako time to dress up and head out for a round of visits to the offices of magazines for which she writes or would like to.

Parks within walking distance of where we live are all small and so heavily used that they're paved or trampled to caked dirt. There is no grass. They have swing sets and slides, sandboxes and fountains, monkey bars and all the stuff necessary to make a child happy. But there's never a lawn where I can sit and watch while Kosumo cavorts.

One of these parks, very near some main defense establishment, so there is regular overhead traffic in helicopters, has a tiny pond. It's her favorite park because the sandbox is biggest. It's my favorite because I can sit in the sand near her, play with her when she wants me to or keep an eye on her when she makes friends with other kids and would rather play with them, and watch the fishermen who pester the silvery fish in the muddy pond.

Theirs is astoundingly technical fishing. We fly fishers feel ourselves somehow superior in our methods. One fellow drives daily to that pond, in the center of that vast city, on a motor scooter. He unbungees a flat aluminum case built to fit on the back rack, walks with it down the rock-terraced bank, and opens it to reveal more complexities than I'd ever carry on a fly-fishing trip to South America. The case itself folds open and has extendable legs. It becomes a table, which he sets solidly on the bank. At the end opposite the water, he folds out a tiny chair a bit like a bicycle seat. At the right side is a rod holder that cups his telescoping graphite rod as delicately as a down bed might cradle it. His bait bucket hangs from a hook to the left side, in easy reach. His tackle box is built into the top of that table, so that when he unfolds it, there everything is, spread at his fingertips.

He fishes with a tiny stick bobber, suspending a small bait of carefully kneaded dough. Only the top of the bobber protrudes from the water. The visible part of it is about the size of a tooth-pick, painted a bright color for some slight visibility. It's not easy to pick the bobber top out on the surface of the pond, speckled as the water is with fallen leaves and twigs. My favorite angler has solved this problem. At the front of what has become his table, he has installed a long gooseneck arm, at the top of which he has mounted a pair of binoculars, which he then aims at his minute bobber top. He sits on his bicycle seat at one end of the table, leans forward over it with incredible intensity, and stares through those binoculars at his bobber for hours. I've watched him, and I've seen him catch fish, though no more than the scattering of other retirees who sit at the edge of the pond and watch their bobbers more casually and without optical aid.

The fish they catch are chubs, about half a pound, all dragged in quickly and with compliance—a practiced affair on the part of both fish and fishermen—netted carefully, unhooked gently, and returned, flapping feebly, to play this game again. My wife once went down and tried to speak to the intent fellow. He would not relinquish his grip on his concentration. He did not take his eyes away from his binoculars. He ignored her.

In the winter before Kosumo turned two years old, her nap time came regularly during our park time. After she'd played in the sand for a couple hours, I'd change her diaper on a park bench, hold her on my shoulder until she went to sleep, then wrap her in blankets in the stroller and read a novel, or hoist her into a pack on my back and nose around the city streets. One day while she was sleeping and I was hiking, I was surprised to find a small patch of green grass, planted in front of a small condo unit, fenced in so nobody dared step on it. It was a triangle, about ten feet to each side, close-cropped and neatly tended.

I felt as one might feel when walking in woods and coming suddenly onto a deer. It freezes watching you and you freeze to watch it. If you move, it bounds away. If you don't move, it looks for a long time, then slips away. I froze and stared at that patch of lawn. I remained frozen about as long as I'd have done had it been a buck. Finally I eased out of there, realizing that I'd miss dinner if I waited for the patch of grass to make the first move.

A couple winters later, which is now a couple winters ago, Masako and I attended a meeting of her home fishing club, named in irony the River Runts. The meeting consisted of a dinner and bursts of talking and laughter in a smoky bar, no speeches, no slide shows. It was enjoyable. Most of the members, now most of them friends, were businessmen attending right from work, dressed in suits. One stood out. Yasushi Yamamoto was a strapping young man wearing jeans and a plaid flannel shirt. Put him in a similar bar in Montana and you might take him for a river guide. You'd not be far wrong. Masako explained over the noise in the bar that Yashu worked in a fishing store, and after some extensive interpreting, he invited us to go carp fishing in a river nearby.

I was near the end of my stay. Masako and Kosumo would be staying on for a few weeks and returning home later. I had plans to bolt for a float trip down the Deschutes the instant my plane touched Oregon. Although it would be the wrong time of year for even moderately good fishing, I needed that dose of being where the grass was not trampled and there were no buildings in sight. Until that trip happened, I preferred my routine of writing

mornings and taking Kosumo to parks afternoons over a specula-
tive carp trip in Tokyo that sounded for some reason like a snipe
hunt to me. Nothing about it excited me, so I turned it down.

Later that same week Masako and I took the one-hour train
ride from Tokyo to adjoining Yokohama, to visit the offices of a
fly-fishing designer. The visit itself was very interesting, but something we saw on the way made me sit forward in my seat. The
train rushed furiously from station to station, on its way crossing
a half-mile trestle over the course of a river that flowed narrowly
in just a tiny portion of its broad bed. The rest of the floodplain
was overgrown with tall bleached grass and scattered scrub willows. Each bank was built up into a dike, with foot and bicycle
paths down the tops.

The broad space between dikes, the full half-mile width of it
and stretching downstream out of my sight, was open space. The
train got over it in a hurry, so that I had no more than a vague
impression of open space and sky and grass and a river running
through it.

"What was that we just crossed?" I asked Masako.

"I think it was the Tamagawa—the Tama River," she
answered.

"That looks like a great place to go," I said.

"What for?" she asked, surprised. She grew up in Tokyo. Its
confinement is the normal condition of life to her.

"There's open space there."

"I think that's where Yashu was trying to invite us to go carp
fishing," she told me.

I pondered that awhile as we rushed through Yokohama, once
again in the jumbled world of buildings tall and small. It was
almost dark when we traversed that trestle again on the way
home. In the dimming light, the broad riverbed looked tranquil.

"I wonder if that invitation is still open?" I asked Masako.

"I'll call Yashu and see," she said.

She did, it was, and we went.

The drive to the river was quite long, a couple hours, Yashu threading narrow alleys in the company van, touching on freeways and jumping off them, honking his horn through traffic jams in city streets, though it was early afternoon. You'd not want to take the drive to fish the Tamagawa for carp any time around rush hour. We stopped briefly at a minimart for what I thought were snacks, some of which were. Yashu added a couple loaves of white bread to the pile on the counter. A standard loaf of bread in Japan is only four thick slices, so the two loaves amounted to about half the size of one of ours. I thought the bread was part of a late lunch, and it looked like lots to me.

When we finally arrived at wherever we were going, Yashu parked on gravel in a place where Tokyo had tapered off to two- and three-story buildings. I saw no sign of any rivers around. While we pulled on rubber knee boots and assembled our gear— all the finest rods and reels on loan from the great Yashu—I remarked at the sight of a tennis court at ground level, backed up against a minor hill. The only other courts I'd seen were on rooftops. This expressed to me that while we were still in Tokyo, though at its edge, there was an enormous ability to distribute space wastefully right where we were, if some of it could be used for folks to bat balls around.

When we got geared up, I hoisted Kosumo onto my shoulders, and we hiked that minor uprise in the ground. On top, we discovered it to be one of the dikes that bordered the river Masako and I had seen from the train.

Masako and I cross the Cascade Mountains every time we drive to fish the Deschutes, which amounts to about once a week when we're home. We've fished rivers on both sides of the Andes in Chile. In New Zealand we fished rivers on the east flank of the Southern Alps. No view I've ever beheld expanded me more than that from the top of the dike on the Tamagawa in Tokyo, Japan. I

don't need to tell you why. In truth, there were ten-story buildings in the near distance, high-rise condos lining the Yokohama
side of the river. But the key word is *distance;* those buildings were
over there, with half a mile of approximate nature strung out
between me and them.

Yashu and Masako didn't even notice that magnificent view.
They paused for a moment on top of the dike to scout out a route
to the river, then headed right down the other side, toward the
narrow band of water in the center of the broad floodplain. I
stood on top, letting all that space of tall bleached grass, scrub willow patches, and the narrow and supine river seep into me until
Kosumo, eager to catch up with Mommy, sat up in her saddle
atop my shoulders and spurred me on like an old horse.

The view, in reality, was not precisely pretty. A low flood-
control dam spanned the entire half mile of the floodplain just a
couple hundred yards upstream from us, cutting off the view in
that direction. The grass and willow plain, wild from a mild distance as we walked it toward the water, turned out to be littered
with shopping carts, plastic jugs, twisted bicycle frames, and all
those things that accumulate in rivercourses that slice through
cities and coalesce their garbage.

There were other anglers, bait dunkers, sprinkled up and
down both sides of the river downstream from the dam when we
reached the water. They could have been imports from that pond
in the park. They used long rods without reels, dough baits, and
tiny bobbers that sat still in backwaters of the river. Most of them
sat in lawn chairs, and most of the lawn chairs were placed far out
in the shallows of the river. Some of these anglers, like those at
the pond, were very serious about this business of catching whatever it was they were after, although we, with all our activity,
probably appeared to be far more serious about it to them.

I'd like to say we rock-hopped out to our fishing position at
the edge of the river, just at the foot of the dam. The truth is, we

cement-hopped. The banks and bottom of the river were not boulders; they were neatly aligned rows of cement blocks, each a pyramid, each a meter square at the base and a meter tall to the top. These pointed blocks were probably designed along the lines of antitank devices and might have been unused ones. They were very effective antiwader devices. Luckily for us—making our fishing possible and likely what drew Yashu to that location—the bottom structure just adjacent to the dam consisted of square cement blocks, each a couple meters square on top and closely enough spaced that we could hop from one to the other.

These blocks, submerged six inches or so, were our transportation right out to the edge of the center current, which was where we desired to fish. We were forced to take turns fishing, because Kosumo could not go out there, so one of us had to stay back and entertain her.

Yashu rigged us with six-weight rods, floating lines, long leaders tapered to 5X tippets, and white flies of Glo-Bug yarn tied on size 8 hooks: perfect imitations of white-bread chunks. It was all amusing to me and showed no promise, because no fish were visible in this entire broad picture. I didn't care. It was enough to be out amid all that space, boots on and a fly rod in hand, with water to cast over, even if it appeared to be empty.

Before we began fishing, Yashu cement-hopped up to a buttress descending from the dam. He laid out four slices of bread, half of all we'd bought, on the sloped cement there, to begin drying in the feeble February sun. "It will float better when it's dried a little," Masako explained to me, and only then did it seep into me that the bread was lunch for the carp, not us. That seemed fine to me. When you're carp fishing in Tokyo, it's easy to suspend judgments about chumming and other minor immoralities, if indeed they're that. I failed to feel a twitch of remorse.

I took the first turn. Yashu directed me to a position on a cement block about a hundred feet below the dam, where the current from the piddling discharge over the top slowed and formed a current line angling along our front. He hopped to a block about half a cast upstream from me, then began tearing a slice of bread into size-8-fly-size pieces, tossing them as far as he could out onto the water. They drifted slowly down to me, sogged up in front of me, and then subsided slowly as they drifted past me. Within five minutes—this was not fast fishing, I suppose because, in insect terms, the "hatch" was sparse—a nose popped out downstream from me and inhaled a bite of the bread that was still half afloat.

I confess that this rise sent the same shot of excitement through me that the rise of a brown trout to a mayfly dun might. I'm not proud of this, I'm just reporting how I reacted to the sudden sight of that rising carp. I didn't own the way I felt; it owned me.

I cast to the rise. I was far out of practice and didn't have a feel for that rod—it was a bit stout, and the leader was so long and fine for it, the 5X overbalanced by the weight of the size 8 bread fly. I plopped the fly on a straight line right down where the rise happened. It landed with a splat. It didn't drift a foot before drag set in. I didn't see any signs that I'd frightened the fish, but I also didn't see any signs of that or any other fish for another five minutes. Then another rose nearby.

I cast again, blew it again, and saw the wake of the frightened fish flailing out of there. It took a couple others with it. That's when I began to get the sense that Yashu had attracted a pod of carp, and that this fishing for them might be worth taking at least slightly seriously. I reined my attention in from that vast view, took a few practice casts until I'd got the timing of that rod and could place the heavy fly somewhat gently onto the water with some slack in the line and leader. I could see that it would be necessary to present the bread fly on a downstream, slack-line drift, just as I would present a size 20 mayfly dun imitation on a downstream wiggle cast to a selective brown trout rising on the Bighorn River in Montana.

Once I got the bugs worked out of my presentation, I dried the fly and readied the line for a cast. Then I waited on that block, prepared for predation, while Yashu stood upstream from me and doled out a few more bits of chum. A carp rose, I worked out line in graceful loops in the air, aimed the delivery stroke, and laid my rod over while the last loop unfurled and the running line slid smoothly through the guides . . . and Masako shouted something from behind me on shore, which caused me to jerk the rod back, which blew that beautiful cast over my shoulder, which was where I was now looking, certain there was an emergency back there.

Masako was pointing up toward the dam. I looked up there. A couple of crows, in Japan almost the size of our ravens, had descended on the drying bread, knocked one slice into the water, and were, on widely spread and noisily flapping wings, departing with two others. Yashu splashed up and retrieved the remaining slice before a circling and shouting third crow could descend on it and abscond with it.

That surprise raid left us on rations for enticement before we'd managed to catch a single carp. But the carp to which I'd been aiming my cast, before the ravens descended, was still ascending for bits of bread that Yashu had already tossed out.

I set the wiggle cast onto the water ten feet upstream from that protruding snout, fed line into the drift of the bread fly, disciplined myself to wait a bit before striking when the carp came up and inhaled the fly with a satisfied grunt, set the hook like a sledgehammer hitting home, and broke off.

It was Masako's turn. She'd learned from my mistake and didn't break her fish off until it turned and shouldered against her uplifted rod.

Yashu fished then and showed us how it should be done. He cast as nicely as you would need to do it to catch a selective brown trout, fed his downstream drift so neatly that the first carp to see his fly was entirely fooled, set the hook gently, played the brutal fish away from the antitank structures downstream from us, brought it in, held it for photos in his hands. We guessed it at two kilos, between five and six pounds.

"Small one," he said as he released it. We all were excited by that victory. We declared the carp—with its O-ring mouth, big gold scales, and drooping koi tail—to be pretty, which took some bending, on my part, of the meaning of that word. But a big brown trout, to a carp lover, might be ugly as hell.

The pod of carp stayed up and active and in front of us, and we were able to keep them there and apparently happy with more minor baitings, though we had to forgo the sweet rolls we'd bought for our own lunch.

I gentled the next one, kept it away from the pyramids despite its bullish rushes, and was able to hold it in my hands on the cement there beneath the dam. We estimated it at a bit less than three kilograms. At that weight, it was about the size of the biggest brown trout I've caught. You'll just have to believe me when I tell you that a three-kilo carp caught in the confines of Tokyo can be just as satisfying as a brown trout of the same size caught in an expanse of plain many miles wide on the south island of New Zealand. You're not asked, or even encouraged, to share that evaluation. I'd not like the Tamagawa to become overcrowded.

Masako had a string of misses on her next turn, mostly because she tried to set the hook before those placidly feeding carp could get their O-rings sufficiently expanded around the size 8 fly. Once she caught onto it, she hooked two or three before I could catch her attention and shout that it was my turn to fish.

I caught more. Masako caught more. Yashu caught most. We ran out of bread. That ended that.

We threaded our way back through the shopping carts and bicycles to the dike, then sat on top of it to gaze for a while out over the floodplain of the river, before leaving it and becoming enveloped once again in the restricted landscape of the city. As we sat there, me crosslegged and Kosumo happy in my lap, Masako the fishing writer revealed to me a bit of research she'd come across about carp in the Tamagawa.

"You don't want to eat them," she told me, which hadn't been one of my desires. "The river is so polluted that the males are turning into females."

"Hermaphrodites?" I asked.

"What's that mean?"

"Just a word," I said. "Go on about these carp."

She said that one in five or six of the males had developed female traits, and that biologists suspected it was from the concentration of female hormones in the water, either because the sewage system can't handle all the estrogen entering the system, or because the breakdown of plastics and PCBs results in chemicals that resemble female hormones. Some speculate that the level of hormones in the Tamagawa is raised by the number of females in the Japanese population now taking birth control pills.

Masako put it less delicately: "Scientists think the carp are changing sex in the Tamagawa because of chemicals from women's piss."

It made me think of alligators in Florida, whose penile parts are known to be shrinking, though it's not known why, at least to me. In truth, it's probably a trip we're all on.

I might be able to go there again. On the way out, down off the dike, back in the van, driving away from the ground-level tennis court, I noticed a train station jammed among the tangle of two- and three-story buildings, within walking distance of the river. I've tracked it down since; it's Fuda Station on the Keio Line. If I can work out the arterial and capillary system of subways and trains to take me from downtown Tokyo to Fuda Station at its edge, I can go back, all by myself.

I haven't had time to do it. I haven't had boldness to do it. But someday I will. Just knowing it's possible to return to that expanse of river gives me a sense of comfort when I'm in that big city.

I envision myself sitting on the train, rushing from the center toward the edge of Tokyo, boots and vest and broad-brimmed western fishing hat on, fly rod in hand, on my way to catch hermaphrodite carp on a dry fly.

Manhattan Odyssey

Paul Guernsey

Everyone knows that a lot of bizarre things occur in Central Park. Heinous crimes. Extraterrestrial abductions. Sex: conventional, unconventional, bestial. Rats that can play the harmonica. Dog manure that aligns itself with the earth's magnetic field. Rollerblading. Doesn't matter what it is; New Yorkers, of course, have heard and seen it all.

But if you really want to *shock* a few Manhattanites, just tell them you're going *fishing* in the park. At first, they invariably think you're full of it and, after you finally convince them, they're horrified. When they discuss it, the look they give you conveys several layers of reservation: It's illegal. Well, if it's not illegal, it *should* be. There's no fish there, anyway. Even if it's not illegal, why would you *want* to?

Angling in general, on the other hand, evokes a far different reaction. To a New Yorker, it seems to represent a cherished but unrecoverable innocence. Cab driver Douglas Levy, for instance, waxes metaphorical on the subject as he transports me and all my gear to a 60th Street rendezvous with the guy I'll be fishing with.

As a cabbie *and* a native New Yorker, Levy is something of an endangered species, and I feel privileged to listen as he tells me about how, in happier times, he used to fish a lot upstate, using both bait and spinning gear.

"Now I fish different streams and hunt different fields. I fish the streams of New York for fares," he says.

When I half jokingly ask his opinion on catch-and-release, he surprises me by saying, "Oh, I *always* let 'em go. I like to let them know what it's like to experience a miracle." Although this seems to directly contradict several earlier statements involving knives and filets, I'd have to be a literal-minded lout to call him on it.

Yes, you *can* fish in Central Park. You just need a New York State fishing license and a taste for weirdness. There are largemouth bass, some specimens of which are rumored to approach double-digit poundages. The park is certainly a fertile place in many observable—if not always appetizing—ways, and I don't doubt there are some real hogs cruising its eight tiny bodies of water.

Near the front entrance to the Plaza Hotel, on 60th, the liveried doormen give me the sides of their eyes but otherwise deny my existence as I stand there with my vest and waders and a couple of rods. Cops likewise ignore me as they trot past on their way to setting up barricades for the Puerto Rican Day Parade, scheduled for that afternoon. They must be making lots of overtime, those cops, because the world premiere of Disney's *Pocahontas* took place in the park the night before. I'm guessing that many of them are also in bad moods.

Jon Fisher, of the Manhattan fly shop the Urban Angler, coasts in on a bicycle to tell me that Edwin Valentín, a friend of his who's going to show me around the park, is running a little late and he offers to take me across 60th to launch my outing on Turtle Pond. Then he eyeballs my gear and cautions, "You don't really want to do much wading here. The snapping turtles are *huge.*" For some reason, I'm actually relieved to hear this.

Baby rat drowning, I tell myself as I twitch a big-eyed popper across the viscous surface of Turtle Pond, which sits above a handsome stone bridge. The bass, if there are any here, remain unimpressed. *Frog moon-walking on motor oil,* I think. But I don't get a hit. Finally, I spot the blimp-like orange underwater blurs that represent a pod of mutant goldfish and, for lack of anything better to do, I try unsuccessfully to pound one up. Meanwhile, I'm obligated to abort every other cast or so in order to allow some wide-eyed civilian to pass behind me on the sidewalk. I keep searching the passersby for the innocence of Pocahontas, but no one even comes close.

A well-dressed man stops and watches with obvious fascination. "I've never seen anyone fly fishing in here," he says.

"There's some big bass," I find myself assuring him.

"Come to think of it," he says, "I've never seen anyone *fly fishing.*"

Then Edwin appears. He's a short, energetic young man in shorts, a thigh-length Daffy Duck T-shirt (Daffy's carrying a fly rod) and a baseball cap stuck full of colorful bass flies, including several of his own imaginative invention. He carries a fly rod that's ready for action. I'll spend the day depending on not only his fishing knowledge, but his survival instincts.

"OK, you can't use a popper here," he immediately tells me. "Never work. They're always feeding under the water. Leeches are better."

I'm about to change flies when he adds, "It's better on 105th Street anyway. I caught a nineteen-inch bass there on Thursday. Let's go over there."

We set off at a brisk walk for a pond scores of blocks away. Edwin every so often launches himself into the air to peek over bushes at lesser bodies of water we pass along the way. Each duckweed-smothered puddle has several angling stories—involving pickerel and panfish as well as bass—attached to it, and Edwin relates them to me as we walk. He also tells me about himself.

He grew up in the ungentle Bushwick section of Brooklyn, became a graffiti artist and eventually began making $1,000 a week etching designs into the rear windshields of cars owned by people with suspicious sources of income. But after the first of his two children was born several years ago, he realized he'd have a better shot at longevity if he moved out of Bushwick. He relocated to Manhattan, began working part-time repairing bikes with his brother, doing other odd jobs and fishing whenever he could. He picks up new fly patterns and techniques by leafing through the fly-tying books at Barnes & Noble and memorizing the illustrations.

"Before I had a vise, I used to hold the hook in my toes," he tells me. Then he shows me one of his earlier toe-ties—a striped deer-hair popper.

Like the sappy liberal I occasionally am, I ask Edwin if I'm depriving him of part of his heritage by taking him away from today's parade. "Nope," he says. "I never go there. You never know when somebody's gonna get into an argument and start shooting. I like to stay out of trouble." Today, if he weren't with me, he says, he'd be home watching TV and tying flies.

Edwin becomes even more animated when we pass the reservoir, no longer in use; it's surrounded by a fence topped with barbed wire. To a Central Park fisherman, this fence represents the locked gates of Eden: a police scuba diver who once had to search the bottom for a body told Edwin he saw bass down there so big they scared him, and now Edwin can't stop dreaming about them. "If that fence ever comes down, I'll be the first one in there," he says. "You better believe it."

Finally, near 105th Street, at a willow-shaded pond called The Pool, he shows me some fish. First, he drops into a crouch and creeps along the edge of the pond, and after a moment he points out a bass that might run three pounds hovering near the shore—a loitering largemouth that radiates the Bowery Boys attitude so typical of the species. "Here, put this on," he says, and gives me a black leech from his hat. "Throw it right in front of him and strip it slow."

I do as he says, making repeated casts, including several back-casts that almost hit innocent people and gawkers as well as one that ends up wrapped around a lamppost, but the bass ignores my offering and moves back and forth and finally out of sight in the murk. "They're spawning right now," he says. "You have to make them mad." It's a hot day, and it seems to me that the water must seem stuporifically tepid even to a bass. But I remain hopeful.

For the next hour, we find quite a few more fish, some of them good ones, but although we change flies frequently—switching to ever more improbable colors—we can't get them to take. Edwin eventually *does* hook one, loses it, and then spots for me while I fish to a bass that I can barely see.

"Strip it," he says. "Stop. Strip. Go ahead, strip. Stop now." Then: "Set the hook!" I lift the rod and find myself fastened hard to a sunken tire.

"Well, he *had* it," says Edwin.

A surprising amount of hunting-and-gathering takes place in Central Park. Edwin points out a homeless man trying to untangle a snarl of monofilament. "Fishing for catfish," he says. "They eat ducks, too. You better believe it." Homeless people often pester Edwin for the fish he catches; being a catch-and-release fisherman, he refuses to hand over any bass.

We spot a couple of Asian women stripping mulberries from bushes near an entrance to the park, and Edwin says some people scour the park's trickling brooks for the resident crayfish—some of which grow blue shells. "I tell them, 'Leave them there, and there will get to be more,' but they never listen to me."

We walk to a small lake called the Harlem Meer. No sign of Pocahontas here either, but we do pass a disciplined platoon of men, dressed in black, practicing martial arts moves.

"Muslims," whispers Edwin.

Whoever they are, they don't even glance at me as I walk past wearing an outfit in which I am feeling more foolish by the minute.

The water in Harlem is both cleaner and deeper than anything we've seen so far, and we fish here for a time with no success, get hit up for a couple of our gaudier flies by two polite kids who are fishing with a handline, and then decide to have a cab drop us back near the Boathouse Pool for one last shot before calling it a day. I'm already satisfied with the outing: Edwin's shown me some fish, which is all anyone—even a guide—can do, and he's also given me a perspective on both New York and Central Park that I couldn't have gotten anywhere else.

The cabbie, an immigrant from Russia named Gregory Naftalieu, becomes excited when he sees our gear. "Is that for *fly* fishing?" he says.

"Yes," we tell him.

"How much does one of those cost?"

Edwin says, "A good one will cost you one hundred and fifty dollars."

"Where can I get one of those?" asks Gregory. So Edwin gives him directions to the Urban Angler.

At the Boathouse Pool, a man wearing nothing but a pair of white jockey shorts strolls up to us. "Any fish?" he asks.

After Central Park, I return to my hotel for a long, careful shower and then head out to meet photographer Richard Franklin for dinner.

Shortly after Greenwich Village restaurateur Craig Béro began dating Laurie Bernstein, now a fishing-book editor for Simon & Schuster, she told him that she had never met anyone so *besotted* with angling. He remembered that, but weeks later he was unsure of the exact word she had used, and he asked her if she still thought he was *be-speckled*.

So when it came time to establish a fly-fishing "general store" at 422 Hudson Street, next door to his Anglers & Writers restaurant at 420, the name he chose for it was the Be-Speckled Trout.

"I really don't think you'll find the word 'be-speckled' in any dictionary," Béro confesses.

Although the Be-Speckled Trout sells chocolates, teas and pastries as well as vintage fishing gear, books and memorabilia, it is as much Béro's private angling collection as it is a store. He clearly cherishes every item he shows you, from the streamer fly—with telltale red headwraps—tied by Carrie Stevens to the Model 360 Perfection fly reel hand-built by Edward Vom Hofe in the late 1800s and valued at around $5,000.

"When I was growing up in the north woods of Wisconsin, my grandfather had a general store where people would come to tie flies and talk fishing. I said, 'Why can't I do this in Manhattan?'"

In fact, he says, Greenwich Village is one of the few places with enough interest and sophistication to support a restaurant and store with a fly-fishing theme. He owns a second restaurant, the Village Atelier, a short distance away. Béro says that among the people who come to the Anglers & Writers to enjoy the fine angling artwork and elegantly presented cuisine—such as the herb-crusted, fruitwood-grilled arctic char in lemon-caper sauce that he ordered for us—the artistic types tend to outnumber the fishermen. "Down here in the Village, we *do* have a lot of fly-fishing people, actually. But we get a lot of artists and writers. It's the artistic part of the Village."

Béro says he chose the double theme for his restaurant as "a whimsy—two things that I like to do." He explains that he grew up on fly fishing and Hemingway, particularly the story *Big Two-Hearted River,* which took place in a setting much like his own childhood surroundings.

His part of the Village is a good—as well as historic—area for anglers: According to Béro, a decent spring-fed brook trout stream used to run—back in the 1600s, anyway—right about where Hudson Street is now. "It's still there, but it's running underground," he says.

And a few blocks away, at 86 Bedford, sits Chumley's, a former speakeasy where—well after the repeal of prohibition, of course—Lee Wulff, John MacDonald and Dan Bailey used to huddle in a corner booth.

You certainly won't find Pocahontas anywhere around the East River these days. But you *will* find Capt. Joe Shastay and his nineteen-foot Mako Classic.

Shastay, who recently became a Jersey City firefighter, fishes out of the New York Skyport Marina at 23rd Street and FDR Drive. It's a ten-minute cab ride from midtown and, once you're on the boat, it's another fifteen minutes to one of Shastay's favorite East River rips not far from the Triborough Bridge.

Joe anchors up, hands me a greenish Clouser Minnow he has more faith in than the ones I brought and says, "You see where the water starts to get rough over there? You think you can hit that from here? If you can, just let it swing down through." I *can;* I've got a good eight-weight and it isn't really a long cast anyway, but since I'm fresh from a trout trip of several nearly fishless days, I'm really not expecting much. On my second cast, though, a twenty-two-and-a-half-inch schoolie thumps hard and hooks himself. A few casts later, I've got a twenty-three-inch fish. It's at times like these that all past failures fade away, and I start slipping into extreme and multi-faceted self-delusion. I catch myself thinking something like *Even if fishing weren't so damn easy, I'd still be good at it.*

Joe Shastay has been guiding for striped bass and bluefish on the East River and New York Harbor for the past five years. In that time, he's seen two human corpses drifting past him in the current.

"What did you do?" I ask him.

"I called the Coast Guard. The first time, they didn't really believe me. They said, 'What does it look like?' I said, 'It looks like a dead body.' The second time, they came right away."

Shastay deadpans, "I'd probably see more bodies, but most of them are wearing cement overshoes."

Then there was the Gulf War, a period during which the dark-haired Shastay happened to wear an equally dark, full beard. One of his favorite fishing spots is near the United Nations building and, on a single day during the height of the war, he received visits from six different boats representing three different law-enforcement agencies. "They just wanted to see what I was doing," he says matter-of-factly.

Usually life on the river is quieter than that, with the blues and stripers providing most of the excitement. Often, except for the barges and the tugs and the occasional wake-producing Circle Line tour, Shastay has the river almost to himself, and he stays busy guiding from March through the end of December. He says the fly fishing is good in all months except July and August, when the fish are running deep—and that the action *really* picks up in October, November and December, with October being a particularly hot bluefish month. "The end of May is pretty good, too," he says.

Shastay encourages his clients to keep their gear as light as possible—he himself takes stripers with a six-inch weight, and once he even had a guy come aboard with a two-weight. "He caught fish with it, too," says Shastay. "I can usually get the boat pretty close."

The two of us catch several more stripers near the Triborough Bridge, then we head down the East River, passing Manhattan on the starboard side, Brooklyn to port, and out into New York Harbor. The weather worsens, and after I take another striper from beneath a barge beyond the Statue of Liberty, it starts to pour. Joe gives me the option of riding with him all the way back to the marina or getting off immediately on a more or less deserted West Side pier.

I opt for the pier, and he takes me in and maneuvers me over to a rusty ladder fastened against a high concrete wall. He tells me that if the gate is locked once I get to the top, I have only to knock on the nearest door and the lady inside will let me out.

Of course, it turns out that the key is *not* under the mat: The gate is locked, most of the high surrounding fence is topped with barbed wire, and by the time I knock on the windowless wooden door to discover that there *is* no lady, Joe's boat is already hundreds of yards away. It's still pouring and I'm a prisoner.

I'm standing there staring at the fence, slowly making up my mind between trying to pick my way over the top in full raingear and one or two other equally unpleasant courses of action, such as shaking the fence and howling at passersby, when Joe—having seen me standing there like a sheep—reappears and moves me to a *different* rusty ladder. When I get to the top of this one, I see an opening to the street, and I wave down to tell him I'm OK. Just as I'm turning away, I notice something dark obstructing my vision, and when I pull off my glasses to have a look, I find a partially composted rat turd clinging to the right lens.

Seldom have I moved as fast as I do now, in getting rid of that thing—I won't paint a picture here, or describe the noises I make, because none of it is pretty—and then I slosh out to the street and flag down a cab driven by a Mr. Mahmood. Mahmood is not a talkative—or a particularly friendly—man, but at this point that's just fine with me. A few minutes later, just as I'm finally starting to relax, I look up to find us closing fast on a wall of stopped traffic.

"Look out, Mahmood," I say. He hits the brakes just before we plow into the rear of the car ahead of us.

Mahmood and I are unhurt, and the two women in the car we've hit appear to be OK, but for some reason, when I step out into the rain to ask how they are, they start screaming at *me.* Don't *I* know how to drive? Can't *I* see where I'm going? What, have I got *shit* on my glasses, or something? I give Mahmood some money just as the women descend on him—the poor bastard—and then I go squishing off through that giant multicultural Love Fest that is New York City.

Shastay occasionally takes the Circle Line tour so he can answer questions about the big buildings from out-of-towners; that's just one of the ways in which he's different from your standard guide. Also, he's got a degree in biology, which helps him figure out the fish and what they're up to. "I've learned to identify one hundred and fifty to two hundred fish species in the river," he says. "If a fish spits out a piece of bait, I want to know what it is." He also keeps careful records of temperatures and the times of day when the fish are hitting. He's not much of a bird chaser; he'd rather know where the fish are hanging without having to be educated by seagulls.

We fish together morning and evening for two days, and we find stripers on each outing.

On the last night, after fishing the Triborough spot again, we motor down the river past a subdued dinner party aboard the Kennedy yacht, *Honey Fitz*—Joe ignores my pleas to pull up next to it so I can ask them if they're catching anything—and we anchor right at the base of the Statue of Liberty. It's raining again, and the stripers don't seem to be hitting at this particular spot. But the city is shining behind us and the statue *does* bring a lump to my throat, and it's a glorious night just the same.

Holy Water

Art Scheck

Even on its worst day, when the water was mostly hidden by a thick mat of algae and the banks were slimy with the droppings of geese that had forgotten how to migrate, with hoodlums smoking joints in the parking lot and a dozen yuppie matrons screeching at hyperactive toddlers in the play area, the pond in the park still did not qualify as a fisherman's hell. That honor belonged to the nearby river, where a rich stew of industrial pollutants trapped in the mud made the carp sprout tumors right out of a science-fiction flick. To an imagination shaped by a Catholic upbringing, the pond in the park seemed a piscatorial purgatory, a place to which God might consign a sinful angler for a few millennia of suffering before admission to fishing heaven. But it was hardly ever worse than that.

Some days it wasn't too bad at all, this square hole in the ground. It contained water, of a sort, and the water contained fish. When you live deep in the heart of Jersey and have a young family, little time, and less money, you learn to appreciate fish-containing water you can reach in five minutes, depending on traffic.

America's suburbs are dotted with such ponds, the brainchildren of local politicos with a little grant money and relatives in the excavating business. From a fisherman's point of view, ours was better than most. A big fountain in the middle ran nonstop from April until late October, aerating the water and cooling it a little during the summer. From a fish's viewpoint, our pond probably wasn't ideal habitat, but unlike some ponds in neighboring towns, at least it wasn't lethal in July and August.

Years of bucket biology accounted for the mix of fish: largemouth bass, bluegills, pumpkinseeds, a few crappies, and some nondescript minnows, all living in a nice balance of predator and prey. They had plenty of structure—tires, rims, a shopping cart, a doorless oven, a few car batteries, and a couple of fifty-five-gallon drums—next to which they could hide. The larvae of damselflies, dragonflies, and caddis dwelled in the weeds that carpeted the bottom. Somehow little green scuds had ended up in the pond, as I discovered one summer while removing a wad of vegetation from a streamer fly; the weeds were thick with the tiny crustaceans. A handful of frogs managed to breed in the shallows, and a couple of turtles had wandered overland from other ponds and found ours a good place to live. As accidental ecosystems go, this one was pretty healthy.

Once a year, at the end of April, the town fathers dumped in a truckload of hatchery trout for a kids' fishing derby. But the pale, stump-finned trout were aliens, and I was always happy when, the day after the derby, the kids' parents descended on the pond to hoist them out with tackle that could easily have jerked bluefish over the rail of a party boat. That was the only time the pond got any real fishing pressure, and probably as close as any of the suburbanites ever came to wilderness adventure.

Like any body of water, the pond went through seasonal changes. At the start of the fishing season, right after the fountain came on, the water was as clear as a bonefish flat. Then, driven by the suburban passion for grass that makes a putting green look like a slag heap, our public-works authorities drenched the ball fields and lawn with fertilizer. The springtime rains washed most of the chemicals into the pond, where, supplemented by a steady supply of goose poop, they fed the weeds and algae. By the time the sunfish started thinking seriously about making nests, the pond had a fringe of algae. By Memorial Day the weed beds had become impenetrable aquatic jungles and the algae had blossomed into floating mats the size of Cadillac hoods. By mid-June only narrow channels remained between the mats of algae, by then drifting just inches above the tops of the weed beds.

A true Jerseyman loves a green lawn, but he doesn't like green stuff in and on his water. And so, sometime in June, the same municipal experts who had soaked the fields with fertilizer doused the pond with herbicide. Some years they put up little signs warning not to play in the water or eat any fish that came from it; some years they didn't. The algae went away (most of it, anyway), the weed beds shrank, and the water took on a bizarre, metallic bluish green tint for a week or so. Then it cleared up and things went back to abnormal, until the next round of fertilizer.

I once called town hall to note that if the authorities didn't load up the pond with enough artificial plant food to fertilize Iowa's corn crop, they might not have to treat it with enough poison to make Kansas a sterile wasteland. I might as well have spoken in Martian; in the 'burbs, not fertilizing grass is as unthinkable as not calling your mom on Mother's Day. Besides, the only people who ever ate any of the fish were poor folk from the ghetto in the next town. Their three-headed children weren't our problem.

Somehow, the fish and bugs and frogs and turtles survived the annual chemistry experiments. Most of them, anyway. A few sunfish would go belly up, most of the bass would change colors to the pale shades indicative of severe stress, and every now and then I'd catch a fish with an open sore on it. But once the water resumed its normal color, the fish reverted to their usual lively selves. They build things tough in New Jersey, where unnatural selection favors the unnaturally hardy.

Like the fish, I adapted to the environment, mastering skills some anglers never learn. During the peak of the algae bloom, I made pinpoint casts into the narrow channels between the mats of mung, working my fly for a couple feet, and then deftly sliding the line off the glop before the fly picked up a half pound of swamp snot. I learned to appreciate not only flies tied with weed guards, but also those shaped so that they don't collect loose algae on their noses. I learned how to ease off on the pressure when a hooked bass wrapped itself in the weeds, as nearly every one did when the vegetation was thickest, and wait for the fish to extricate itself, as it usually did. Between the green slime in the water and the crust of goose crap on the banks, I became *very* good at cleaning fly lines. And rods, and reels. Shoes, too.

Fishing the pond in the park drove home the importance of a high backcast more forcefully than any other place could have. The challenge wasn't to keep one's backcast out of trees and bushes, because the pond had only a few sickly trees around it. But it had paved walkways on three sides, set back six to forty feet from the water. It does not do, in a prosperous burg thick with lawyers, to hook a jogger on the backcast. He resents it, particularly if he is not a brother of the angle. Far worse is to sling a low backcast and foul-hook a tyke speeding by on a Big Wheel tricycle. While it's probably true that few sporting thrills can rival the first reel-searing run of a five-year-old with good legs, the thrill would fade when the game's mommy called the cops and then her lawyer.

I'd grown up fishing small streams where I had to make low casts. At the pond, I became a master of reaching for the sky with forty feet of fly line. If people who run fly-fishing schools held them in busy suburban parks, we'd have fewer inept casters.

For four years I fished the pond in the park mostly because it was there when I didn't have time to go someplace better. I miss it now only when I've had enough to drink to make me nostalgic about the world in general. Still, the place had its moments. Three opening days running, it gave me an alternative to facing the barbarian hordes that jam New Jersey's trout streams before daylight. I'd drive over to the park at a civilized hour in the late morning, catch a couple of big crappies on a streamer or wet fly, pronounce the season well and officially started, and go home to have lunch and watch the Mets. You can't beat that for an opening day.

Thanks to the aeration provided by the fountain, the bass rarely sought refuge in the deeper water, and I could usually catch at least a couple on the surface any evening from May until mid-August. One Fourth of July evening, with only an hour until it would be time to take the kids to the fireworks, I landed a dozen keeper-size bass in fifty-eight minutes by the watch, all on a homemade deer-hair bug. In terms of bass per hour, that Independence Day remains my second-best evening of fishing.

On sunny spring days the sunfish would gather under the moribund willow tree that leaned over one corner. It was, as golfers say, a difficult lie. My only angle of attack put me on the edge of a blacktop trail, with a couple ragged trees and two usually occupied benches behind me. Every backcast involved swiveling my head to make sure I wasn't going to hook a jogger, a branch, a toddler, or a snoozing octogenarian taking the sun. Then the forward cast had to miss the overhanging willow branches. Sometimes I could pluck twelve or fifteen fat bluegills from under the willow before the rest of the fish wised up. Well pleased, I'd go home to nurse a sore neck.

Despite the noise and pesky brats and general grubbiness of the place, the pond grew on me over the years. Objectively, it had nothing to recommend it except fish I could usually catch. But when the nearest running water that *might* have held a trout or smallmouth was half an hour away, depending on traffic, and the nearest wild trout might as well have been in China, that was a lot.

In time, a fisherman can have proprietary feelings even for a square excavation in a grubby, ugly suburban park. You follow the progress of each spawning season, wishing the fish success in their conjugal efforts. The daily accumulation of fresh litter becomes a personal affront. An exceptionally loud boom box in the parking lot qualifies as a public disturbance that the cops should quell with truncheons and tear gas. The fertilize-then-poison cycle comes to represent our general idiocy in environmental matters.

Besides, I couldn't help admiring the pond's inhabitants. Fish that live in pristine wild places have done nothing to earn my respect. They're *supposed* to grow big and fat and become the parents of many broods. But the fish in my pond had to beat the odds every day. Maybe they were mutants, but they were tough mutants, and they were *my* mutants.

Or maybe I just have a perverse fondness for what an acquaintance once described as "urban ditch fishing." It's a harmless aberration. And it does leave the nice places free for anglers who can't make the grade in grittier environments.

The pond in the park had one drawback: it rarely offered solitude, that most precious ingredient of good fishing. To enjoy any peace and quiet, I had to fish the pond early in the morning, before the suburban frenzy began its daily assault on reason and the senses. At six o'clock in the morning, sometimes the pond let me forget where I was fishing, at least for an hour. Until lawn mowers and weed whackers commenced their hellish racket and horns began blowing on the main drag, before the first gang of fathers arrived to bellow profanity at the umpires or referees officiating at the morning's first game, I could almost pretend that my casts were dropping into wild waters.

My wife and I had a typically grueling suburban Saturday in the works. The girls, then ten and seven, needed to be a dozen different places: birthday parties, painting lessons, gymnastics rehearsals, First Holy Communion class, more parties, scout meetings, dance class. The lawn and hedges, as the landlord had noted seventeen times in the past five days, needed attention. The refrigerator and pantry needed restocking, a chore that would entail a visit to the birthplace of road rage, a New Jersey supermarket on a weekend. By day's end each of our vehicles would have another eighty miles on its odometer, nearly all of them racked up in second or third gear. Parenthood in the 'burbs is hell on clutches.

Perhaps a better man could face such a day without spiritual preparation, but I knew I'd need to fish for an hour before diving into the maelstrom. As I set the alarm on Friday night, I asked Mary Jo if she'd like to come with me to the pond. She elected to sleep in till seven, rationing her strength for the ordeal Saturday would bring. I promised to make as little noise as possible in the morning.

As I turned onto the main drag at ten to six, the Greek who owned the corner deli and adjoining liquor store was just beginning to sweep up the broken glass left in his parking lot by the previous evening's gathering of drunken teenagers. The church parking lot was empty, as was the lot at the Italian restaurant rumored to be a mob hangout. The gates of the cemetery were still locked. Where I turned left onto the park road, I had to wait for only three cars after the light changed. Lawn mowers dozed in garages; commuters slept through a morning without a rush hour.

The park was empty, the pond asleep under the perpetual rain of the fountain. Birdsong filled the air, and a couple of bunnies scampered into the brush at the edge of the soccer field. Downright bucolic, considering the setting.

Most anglers develop rituals. I knew I'd start with a deer-hair bass bug with grizzly hackle legs, but I always waited until I reached the water before tying on a fly. It's presumptuous to pick out a fly before looking at the water. And though it probably made no difference where I started fishing, when I had a choice I usually began at the far left-hand corner and fished clockwise around the pond. In the morning, that really was the best way to begin, since I'd have the sun at my back. And it was somehow important to get as far away as possible from the parking lot and street.

I made a wide detour around the edge of the pond and walked softly to the corner. A little bass scooted away as I approached; a big bluegill held its ground, turning to face me. A fish swirled about sixty feet away. For early June, the algae was unusually sparse—a couple of doormat-size clumps floating around, and a strip about the size of a hallway runner against the shore in front of me. Maybe a relatively dry spring had allowed most of the fertilizer to stay on the grass. Another fish swirled, this one against the bank nearest the parking lot. Clearly, the deer-hair bug was indicated. I studied one fly box, and then another, to find a bug I liked the looks of best.

After tying on the bug, I looked up and saw that I no longer had the place to myself. An elderly Asian gent dressed in a black jogging outfit and white sneakers had materialized on the bank nearest the parking lot, almost diagonally across from me. He was standing on the little pavilion where teenage couples smooched in the evening and from which politicians harangued the assembled masses after parades. The pavilion had a six-foot wall at the back, which shielded sparking couples from the view of folks in the parking lot, and two steps at the front that led to the water. It was an ugly structure without any apparent purpose, and I always assumed it was the work of a councilman with kinfolk who sold pressure-treated lumber.

Well, I thought, perfect solitude is probably too much to ask for, even at six in the morning. At least the old guy hadn't brought a boom box or a radio-controlled toy speedboat or any of the other infernal contraptions with which people chase the silence that might encourage contemplation. Reflection is not a big pastime in most of America, probably because it leads to depression.

The old man nodded to me, and I nodded back. I began fishing.

It felt good to cast. I started throwing long double-hauls down the shoreline, dropping the deer-hair bug next to the mat of algae that lay along the bank, working it slowly for twelve or fifteen feet, then picking up the line and firing another cast. As the bug was sitting still, I glanced over at the old Chinese guy on the pavilion. He had begun some sort of exercise routine, a series of graceful and elaborate movements that looked like a warmup for a martial-arts contest. Tai chi, I guess.

A fish swirled on my bug and I missed the strike, pulling the fly into the algae mat in the process. I stripped in the bug to clean off the glop, took a few steps down the bank, and resumed casting. The old guy continued his tai chi. He seemed good at it, at least to my unschooled eyes, and completely oblivious of my presence.

Over the next twenty minutes I fished my way down the back bank almost to the corner without getting another strike. Strange. Maybe the fish didn't want the bug this morning. Or maybe the angle of the sun was driving them out of the shallows along the back bank. I swapped the hair bug for a little Deceiver tied with a marabou tail, a fly with which I could work the middle depths a few yards out from the bank. The old guy kept on exercising, facing the sun as he went through his seemingly endless routine.

I fished the Deceiver carefully at the corner, where I could almost always find a bass. Not this morning. I threw a few casts toward the middle of the pond, out to the edge of the spray from the fountain, on the theory that some of the bass and most of the crappies might be holding deep. Nothing doing in the middle, either.

After I turned the corner, I was only about a hundred feet from the pavilion. The elderly gent was still at it. I wanted to fish the bank all the way to the next corner, the one by the pavilion, but I didn't want to invade the old guy's space. On television, I'd seen hundreds and even thousands of Chinese folk doing tai chi together, but exercise has always seemed to me a personal, private business. And this old guy was all by himself, doing his silent thing in the early morning sun. Approaching within casting distance seemed rude somehow. So I changed flies again to kill time, switching to a big, black Woolly Bugger tied with some lead under the body. If they don't want white, try black.

They didn't want black. I took a few steps, made a half dozen casts spread over a ninety-degree arc, and took another few steps. My best double-haul could have dropped the fly right at the bottom step of the pavilion, three feet in front of the old guy, who seemed to have picked up the pace. Was he *ever* going to stop? Was he in training for the tai chi Olympics or something?

I knew that I had to knock off by seven o'clock. Duty called. And I hadn't hooked a fish.

At ten to, the old guy finally quit. He bowed to the pond, slowly, and then nodded to me again. Then he walked away.

Last chance, and the clock was running. Decision time. The corner by the pavilion had some good, four-foot-deep structure—several tires and a big truck rim—that usually held a bass, but maybe the old man's tai chi gyrations had spooked the fish there. I'd be better off hustling to the last corner, where the decrepit willow tree leaned over the water, and trying to catch a bluegill or two on a small fly. I reeled in my line and started walking, fumbling in a vest pocket for the panfish-fly box. A gray soft-hackle wet should do the job, I figured.

As I turned the corner, I noticed that the water in front of the pavilion looked funny. Dark, but somehow shallower. When I got within ten feet, I saw why: I was looking at the backs of dozens and dozens of fish about a foot and a half below the surface. They weren't stacked up in neat rows, but they were all facing the same direction, toward the spot where the old Chinese man had been exercising. Bluegills, crappies, and bass, including a couple of bruisers, made a dense, wedge-shaped school pointing at the pavilion. Many dozens of fish—maybe a couple hundred—were just sitting there, mouths and gills working, pectoral fins slowly waving, staring at the place formerly occupied by the tai chi enthusiast.

You don't read magazine articles about stuff like this happening in Montana or Alaska. But at least I had found the fish.

I backed up a few yards, stripped some line off the reel, and flipped a soft cast at the edge of the school. I overshot my mark, and the fly landed well inside the crowd of fish. They should have spooked, but they didn't. As I stripped line, six or eight fish moved to get out of the Woolly Bugger's way, then calmly resumed their positions, still facing the spot the old man had occupied. The slinky, black fly swam away from the school without a single fish in pursuit.

I'm not big on mysticism or metaphysics. I don't even go to church. I don't do a whole lot for the good of my soul. Except, of course, fish. But it occurred to me that maybe I should just leave these fish alone, that perhaps I had stumbled across some sort of cosmic hatch beyond matching, or even understanding, by the likes of me.

Besides, they didn't seem too hungry that morning.

So I let my fly sink to the bottom and just stood there, watching. After a few minutes the school began to disperse, a few fish around the edges turning and moseying off down the shoreline or vanishing into the deeper water out by the fountain, then a few more.

What did the old guy know? What the hell had he really been doing?

A lawn mower roared to life in a nearby yard, its owner flipping the bird at the town's noise ordinances. A long screech of tires out on the main drag ended with the blaring of two horns.

Two minivans full of kids in baseball uniforms pulled into the parking lot and took the spaces on either side of my truck.

I had things to do. I wished the fish good luck and split.

Mary Jo was making breakfast for the girls when I got home. She asked how the fishing had been.

"Different," I said.

"Catch anything?"

"I'm not sure."

I'm still not. But I wish I'd run after the old guy and caught up with him and asked for a lesson.

Downtown Stripers, Oaktown Angst

Seth Norman

I argue with myself about the ethics of writing "where-to" articles and books. Not this time, however: Here's the offer of a "where-to," a place where two (2) anglers at a time can catch stripers from one pound to thirty. Remote? Downtown Oakland. Dangerous? Maybe, but not the way it was once.

I write this with full expectation that I will rarely again find unoccupied the space I want here at the time I want it. Two things supersede my gross self-interest:

John Ryzanych, owner of Icon Products, believes publicity will benefit his efforts to make Lake Merritt and its estuary part of a superb and unique urban fishery; and,

Poachers.

But first . . .

The strike is silver—a broad shock of bright light sparking in brown water. The tail flashes toward the surface, and for an instant

I see part of the striper in three dimensions—parallel black lines arching along a flank, crisp edges of fins.

Gone. But a second fish rises nearly straight up, takes a tiny smelt from the edge of a current seam, then plunges straight down.

It's a metal and feather meal.

"Got 'im," John says.

Oh yes.

I first fished this pool twenty-five years ago, despite cautions from a cop friend. "Guy was shot in the Laney College parking lot right across from where you want to stand," on a walled platform below the 7th Street bridge, inland from I-880 and the railroad trestles. "I wouldn't go there at night unless I'm carrying a gun," he vowed. Then, because he did go there at night with a gun, "But those stripers come in, believe it."

I did believe. I'd seen them—or seen some *things* fracturing the reflection of moonlight when I walked this way to the college sculpture barn, winter nights after long days I'd spent working cash-on-the-barrel labor for contractors in Berkeley. Real animals—the contractors, I mean; but those were also big beasts ripping their heads around out there in the current, creating the kind of swirls that suck holes in the surface of moving water.

Fresh water, I wrongly presumed for a long time, thinking the players must be giant carp, rolling the way I'd watched them in the Allegheny River. Naturally I intended to investigate in better light. But by the time I'd finished picking out a broken sewer main or muling chunks of concrete, stopping to shower off, then humping a half mile to catch the BART downtown . . . I always ended up crossing the bridge well into dark. Inevitably my aching shoulders would tighten under my coat; the walk made me edgy as an anchovy. I suspected then what my cop pal would later confirm—that pretty as the pool might look, this was not a nice place.

It looks rather better today. Lined on both sides by strips of grassy park, it's really a broad spot in the channel that runs into Lake Merritt from the Bay at high tide and out with the ebb. Along the bank stand faintly annoying abstract structures that testify to the prescience of my sculpture teacher way back when, an avowed enemy of representational art (which was the only kind that interested me). Perhaps it's on these grand pieces that local squatters relieve themselves these days, because the dark walkway under 7th Street doesn't reek of urine as much as it did in the late 1970s.

We hit stripers back then, once in a while. But in all my previous visits put together, I'd never seen so many as John and I had, middle of a bright August afternoon.

"See what I mean?" he calls from the mud strip where we have been landing fish. "Been like this for a month now. I get four fish, six, even seven a session. I've seen thirty-pounders from up on the bridge, though the biggest I've landed is eight or ten. Plus those steelhead, up to four pounds. Incredible, isn't it?" I watch him a moment, see the fish run line off his reel. "This one ain't bad, I'll tell you that."

I nod, turn, flip my fly and yarn indicator back up into a moving wall of water below the grate that screens the gate above.

Indicator, that's right: we're high-sticking stripers. Four feet beneath mine is suspended a minute streamer. I'd heard of techniques like this before, once from a guy who uses white jigs in a reservoir, also for stripers; another time from an angler who's tried something similar on trout. But John and his friend Dave Hickson have been actively experimenting with this tactic lately. Hickson has all kinds of experience with indicator techniques; he and Dean Schubert, now of Orvis, helped popularize this style of nymphing in Northern California, then on several Northwest steelhead rivers.

Bobbers, some call them. But as is often the case, the greased yarn we're using at the top end of this pool, where water flows out from under the bridge through a grate, serves better to suspend the fly than as a tattletale. The stripers look up for the baitfish we're imitating; they lie in ambush below a tongue of current, then rip toward the surface to attack. Because I *see* most strikes, I can mark how often good hits don't even twitch the yarn. Because of slack created by currents? Because a striper can "spit" so quickly?

The situation changes if the fly drifts downstream from where we stand. Then the changing angle of light usually renders both fly and flash of fish invisible; from there on, the indicator does serve as bobber—though how reliably, I have to wonder.

Most strikes, however, come from fish lurking close behind the grate. That's where John took the fish he's fighting, last of three, and where I hooked one of a pair. But the grate, which screens a gate through which the water travels, is only ten or twelve feet wide. A quick flip is all you need to make for a cast, but it's only possible from a space barely wide enough for those two anglers I mentioned.

There are four of us right now. John and I arrived about ninety minutes ago, to wait on the changing tide; an hour later we were joined by a pair of spin fishers, who set up ten feet down from us. There's not another fisher visible in the hundred yards of both banks in front of us, but we four stand within a leader length of each other. À la Dillinger, "Because that's where the fish are."

The spin fishers have now seen John and me land four stripers between us and have themselves hit nothing. They exchange looks when we release fish. Early on, John and I discussed the levels of mercury and heavy metals known to exist in striper flesh. We shook our heads about the warnings in Fish and Game regulations, which we suspect are inadequate; we speculated on the long-term effects of dioxin and PCB exposure on children.

Like that. We were talking to each other much too loudly. Our neighbors, however, appeared not to notice.

Polite? Or is this "Hear No Evil"?

How about "Eat No Evil?" A week before this episode, a *San Francisco Chronicle* article noted the suspension of Oakland's "Fishing in the City" program, a get-kids-off-the-streets affair that stocked trout and rented tackle in a net-enclosed portion of Lake Merritt. Dead birds forced the issue: between two and five had showed up tangled in monofilament. This is of special concern, since the lake is a federal wildlife preserve. But exactly where the birds encountered the line is anybody's guess, as John points out, and the kids' program "kept track of every hook and sinker."

Another question John poses is whether fish, or the birds themselves, were the intended prey. Oakland is rumored to have occasional problems with another program, unofficial, which could be called "Trapping Birds in the City." That should invite discussion of a subject the *Chron* article only mentioned in passing—what it politely called "subsistence fishing on the lake, practiced predominantly by some Asian American residents of the community."

John isn't keen on the identification of any one group as the problem. He also resents the term "subsistence": "I don't think any of the folks fishing out here use the lake as a primary source of food."

God help them if they do. Almost ten years ago an employee of an East Bay park district told me the park officials knew about tests conducted on stripers caught a few miles away from the site I'm fishing. He said the levels of mercury discovered were truly frightening—way beyond what anyone expected—and he promised that the results would be released soon.

Didn't happen, as far as I know. But another *Chron* article a few days after the kids' program story described the ongoing and worsening effects of nonpoint source pollution (that which is transported by water to pollute another locale) in the Bay from organophosphate pesticides, mercury, dioxin, polyaromatic hydro-carbons, and PCBs. Ultimately the problem is not any one of these, say scientists, but "is probably all of them combined, each working in malign concert with the other."

Although the article is mostly about marine life, the implications for humans are obvious.

Despite the questionable wisdom of consuming the local striped bass, harvesting these fish continues, by methods mostly not legal. John says he cuts down a trot line "about once a week" from the little section of water he fishes, and sees snaggers converge on the gate at night. A deputy sheriff told him that two years ago officers found a gill net stretched across the channel. And the taking of juvenile fish is routine, as is the tendency to kill as many fish as can be caught, with one or two individuals "filling limits" for people who stop by to transport carcasses up to cars on the street.

It galls me to hear that. It's a system I saw used endlessly at Lake Temescal, before the Oakland fire, where I began to take poaching rather personally. Awesome to see what sixty or eighty people can do to a three-acre lake, fishing from dawn to dusk, killing a limit for every adult and child in their party, then hauling the fish up to cars that drive away and return empty, so that the process can begin again.

Awesome is only one of the words that might describe such carnage. There are others. Less than three months ago, while walking Sophie and Max around that little lake, I met an angler leaving "from pure disgust" at what he'd seen people doing to bass on their spawning beds. I asked him if he'd called the park police; no, he said, because the culprits had taken their kill and gone home.

Maybe those culprits were gone, but a hundred yards up the path I found a teenager trying to rip a sow bass off her bed with a naked jig hook, at least a 4/0.

The youngster and I and his three older friends had a nose-to-nose discussion. A cop did come and, with a little help, found the jig. He apologized to me because he could not arrest the vermin—he found no fish—but I took the opportunity to assure my fellow citizens that on my next walk I'd be carrying a camera, and hoped to someday have the chance to display their faces to as much of the world as would look.

One likes to think it would make a difference.

"How's this?" calls John, holding up a fish of five, maybe six, pounds. He releases it. The two other anglers look at each other. I flip the fly up toward the grate, and two seconds later comes the flash.

Deeply does my eight-weight bow. I will break this one off. Eventually.

"The thing is," says John soon after, "that the potential here is so fantastic, and everything's already in place." He pauses. "What I mean is, it will cost almost nothing to improve conditions here and create what really could be tremendous. Imagine, just imagine—*Oakland,* with a world-class urban fishery."

I *can't.* But for a year now, John has been exploring the potential of Lake Merritt and this channel. Which really is impressive. One of the last natural salt lakes on the San Francisco Bay, Merritt hosts enormous numbers of anchovies, topsmelt, gobies, sticklebacks, even a few stripers. A 1966 study John faxed me reveals that it once held also, and may now, surfperch, killifish, Pacific herring, threadfin shad, bat rays, leopard sharks, and "salmon or trout." Along with these is the invertebrate life to sustain them: tubeworms, mussels, clams, oysters, shrimp, and crabs.

"All right," I say. "What exactly do you want to happen?"

John thinks an instant. "The first thing is to improve the water quality in the lake generally—that benefits everybody. Then, add the welfare of fish and other marine life forms into discussions about Merritt, especially as they involve flows at the gates. Because when the gates are closed for long periods—to manipulate the water level for certain boating events, for example—stagnation sets in. I've seen the kills, all these bodies of putrefied baitfish spilling out when the gates open again. The idea isn't to put a stop to those manipulations, necessarily, but to time them, consider the effects, and mitigate whatever damage might occur.

"The next thing is to address the grates over the gates. They're already scheduled for work; so before it's done, let's consider the size of the openings, maybe adapt them to let larger fish through. If we can do that, spread the stripers through the system, that will also expand the fishing opportunities. The more people fishing, the less chance for poachers to wreak havoc.

"Of course, we need to know more. These steelhead, for example; are they returnees from plants in Merritt? And what effect will it have, if any, to allow in more anadromous fish?"

Already, John asserts, he knows of those who will volunteer to conduct studies, sample steelhead habitat. He's met with representatives from agencies with interests at the lake, including the City of Oakland Aquatic Sports Groups, the Lake Merritt Institute, that "Fishing In the City" program, the Alameda County Department of Public Works. He finds them "more than receptive—eager."

"I'll tell you what I'd like," John says, laughing. "I'd like to sit down with Jerry Brown and present all this to him. . . ."

I can see that. I can even see Mayor Jerry Brown accepting the invitation. If I squint, I can envision an Oakland Chamber of Commerce poster: sunset on Lake Merritt, the shore ringed with lights, skyscrapers in the background . . . and an angler in silhouette, fly line unfurling against the crimson horizon. The inset shows a striper or steelhead, with a caption reading "Oakland, where business and pleasure meet at the lake."

Could happen.

Like hell, I think; and while listening to John, I suddenly hear a dim refrain, gray at the edges. I can't quite remember how it goes: "If you won't stand with me, then get out of my way."

That's about right. John believes in this, can see it all come together, is willing to donate time, help facilitate, coordinate communication among the various agencies. I don't believe, not because what he says is anything but reasonable, but because after living in Oakland as long as I have, and learning more than I should, I am so weary of this town that I am certain it could screw up a Second Coming, that it can and will inevitably pervert and exploit and probably brutalize the most failsafe and beneficent scheme. To look into Oakland long and hard enough—the school districts, the nepotism, the violence—*should* turn a decent person to salt. "I'm from Oakland," I tell people when they ask, "but I've done nothing wrong."

That isn't how John feels. Nor is it the way lots of other people feel, all of whom are probably much nicer than me. The hard fact is that anybody who feels the way I do will never try to change anything.

John will.

So just stay out of his way.

Half an hour later I watch him land a striper of fifteen pounds. And I would feel brighter, except for this:

While John is taking these fish on elegant little flies he ties, both he and Hickson, who's also an enthusiastic conventional fisher, have experimented with tiny "plastics" that can either be thrown with a fly rod or incorporated into traditional patterns.

Deadly stuff. And the spin anglers, standing near to me, hoping to catch a fish, are both rigged with exactly the kind of tiny plastic lure Hickson once showed me—the very brand Dave says is hard to find. They have not caught on to indicators yet but are getting a lesson today that I know they won't forget.

John knows the men. They kill what they catch, but he doesn't know if they are among those who pass fish after fish up to people in cars on the street. Still, every time I see one of those little lures at the end of one of their lines . . . I feel slightly ill. It would just be *so Oakland,* I think, for poachers to take a page from a catch-and-release fly fisher's book and, with it, *slaughter* fish.

That's what I think. But I'm not the one who'll change things.

John might be. As I'm writing this, he calls. Laughing.

"Eleven," he says. "I landed eleven there yesterday afternoon. And they are getting bigger."

Post note: Seth Norman comes by his Oakland attitude honestly: In 1990, he authored and coauthored a series of articles about corruption in the Oakland Housing Authority Police Department. A third of that force was indicted by a grand jury. The story ran twice on "60 Minutes." Seth was nominated for the Pulitzer Prize, and he won the Golden Medallion Award of Special Merit in Public Interest Journalism from the State Bar Association and the Jane Harrah Award in Print Media from the Bar Association of San Francisco.

THROUGH THE ICE

Pete Fromm

My daughter's house. Four stories, for crying out loud. Her and her husband. I can just see them thinking, Let's see the Joneses keep up with *this*! Dug into the side of a hill that'd wind a goat. Covered with gingerbread like it's a couple hundred years old. Neo-Victorian, Carolee told me when I first stood gaping in the drive—a drive so steep it's the one thing they do need their Land Rover for.

Makes me plain embarrassed to be living here. Every time I catch a glimpse of it.

But the drive, I have to admit, is what saves me. The lake's only a block from here, and after I jury-rigged a wheel setup, I can get a running start—hell, a bobsled run—and make it damn near there, depending on how well the street's been plowed. Dump the wheels then, and start dragging it on the runners.

I left the big ice house back home, of course, along with most everything else when they brought me out here to live with them. I couldn't drag it anymore anyway. But Jerrod—I swear that's his real name, our only child's husband—has a full woodworking shop beside the garage. I don't know what it's for, more keeping up with the Joneses, but my first winter out here I built this new ice house while they were both out at work. A collapsible one, like we had to make for the reservation back home, where they didn't allow any houses left on the lake. First sawdust that shop ever saw. Big, giant, empty, childless house. It's like a movie set of a home. What do they think they're working *for*?

There's only room in the ice house for me, which is plenty, given the crowds of friends I've got left. Them not dead are as good as to me, to hell and gone in Montana, or even Arizona. And half of *them* in homes, guys who spent most of their lives under the stars. Could make me cry, though I know they don't think I'm any better off, dragged off here to Minnesota by my daughter the hotshot lawyer.

And I tell you, cutting out that single trapdoor in the floor was a pretty strange feeling. Knowing I'd be hunched over this hole, watching that world down below me, my lips sticky shut and gummy from disuse. Like they are most times—what the hell do I have to say to a fellow named Jerrod? A financial analyst or some such. I know living with the father-in-law wasn't his idea when he met Carolee, but it sure wasn't mine either. And I know that's just how he plays it at their cocktail parties or whatever it is they spend their lives doing—the long-suffering, saintly martyr. I can see him lifting his champagne or martini or whatever, hear his clogged-nose baritone, "Some days I find his ice house halfway up our street, have to haul it home myself before it causes an accident." See him shaking his head, that rueful smile. Somebody asking, "An ice house? Is that rather like an igloo?" Well, you can just shove your Wall Street bulls and bears straight up your Boston ass.

Pressing the button to the garage door, a button for Christ's sake, lets in a howler. I'll give them that; they've got real weather here. Snow swirls into the big, empty bays, and I duck deeper into my coats. My circulation is barely enough to keep me alive, let alone warm. I'm thinking of buying some of those battery socks. Wouldn't the boys just shit if they ever got wind of that?

The drag out to the lake comes close to finishing me, every time. But the bobsled kickoff to it is damn near as hard on my heart, and I hope that's what takes me. Hooky-bobbing down this grove of new mansions on top of a one-man ice house, dead as a mackerel. I wouldn't mind that at all. Wonder who the hell they'd hire to take care of that little mess.

Once over the curb, then the jogging path—I know, I can barely believe it either—I weave it through the evenly spaced gaps between the maples—they even all turn color, the *same* color, at the same time. Some serious genetics money pissed away on these trees, let alone that they must have brought them in here damn near full grown.

John and I used to drive two hours to haul our house across the wind-blasted ice of the Blackfeet Reservation. Nothing but a few snow-crusted cows for a hundred miles. Now if I get out early enough, the place is almost as deserted, but hell, there's streetlights.

Drilling the hole takes a long time anymore, and if it wasn't so blessed cold, I'd take more than one rest. I'd spring for a gas auger, too, but the noise would bring howls. Now I'm this quaint little oddity, I know that. "Are you on that lake with that cute old man, the one with the house, on the ice?" But let me pull the cord on an auger some five A.M. and the novelty would be gone before I cut through ten inches.

With the snow and the dark, you can't see anything out here, not the ring of mansions, the jogging path, the distant peaks of their great shiny metal and glass towers of commerce. Nothing but the double row of streetlights through the bare branches of the maples, glowing white balls, shot through with snow, which, I have to admit, is kind of pretty in its own way. Not the same as the ghostly glow of a few canvas houses, lantern-lit from inside, all holding guys you know, though you don't know which ones yet, won't till it's light, till there's a lull that'll send people out visiting. But it is kind of pretty, and I don't mind looking out that way till I can get the hole drilled, the hut stood up, the snow shoveled around it to block off light and wind both. Then I dodge inside and get the propane heater going as fast as I can. Little as it is, the house warms up fast, and it's not long before I can take off a jacket, maybe two.

When I go home, in the daylight, when I can see, I don't look around any more than I have to. The illusion won't hold up to that. Pissing, too. What with the prostate, it's once an hour, if that good. Wound up bringing a bucket. With a lid. So I don't ever have to go outside, get slapped by the sun, the skyline, the ring of insane joggers, the Sunday drivers in their BMWs.

But once I get settled, get warm enough to pull off my mitts, I start rigging, picking a sparkle purple hula skirt today, on a lead-head jig, a maggot or two. I have to drop down the magnifier on my glasses to tie it all on, hell, even to stick the maggots—me, who used to tie batches of #20 Tricos for the Missouri or the Snake. By the time I get it all done, I know the day is full on outside, and I know the ice will light up the lake beneath me.

That's when I crack my thermos. Set a steaming cup on the rail, sit back a second with that smell, listening to the good, steady hiss of the propane, the orange glow of its coils—nothing like the tiny wood stove we used to use, John and me, but damn happy all the same.

I work my left leg out of the way and reach down for the trap. My heart's stopped its hammering by now, but I can feel it quicken just a beat or two every time I lift that door, reveal that whole new world. Never ever once guessed I'd be so aware of every beat of my own heart.

Then I flop the door back and let myself look.

The lake's glow is greenish, almost silver green, with the sky bright with flurries. Kind of like the underside of aspen leaves. After a blow starts them quaking. I look down through the water, see the old branches thick with algae, the little flitting bits of life, tiny shrimp, larvae of I don't know what all, maybe a darting flash of fingerlings. I don't know how much they've spent on making this lake, don't know what limits they've gone beyond, what with stocking and aeration, probably even refrigeration in the summers, and for once I don't care. Somebody in this sterile-assed model community wanted trout in this pond, and by God, what they want out here, they get. What I hear, the trout man stroked out before the trout were a foot long. In his fifties. Whole life working toward this dream and he pops a blood vessel. Hope he's fishing somewhere. Poor bastard.

What I can no longer even begin to imagine is what it is Carolee wants, what all this is for, what they'll do when they're older. Just keep chasing more money? She once said to me, "Kids? Who has time for kids anymore?" She laughed when she said it. Geraldine would have told me it served me right for prying.

I lower my line. Maybe ten feet to the bottom. Twelve. I've got a good sandy spot, not many sticks, not much for weeds. I crank it up a foot, wait, then give it a jig. Once every thirty or forty seconds. Nothing too constant. Random. Sporadic. Eye-catching.

Thing is, I never was much of an ice fisherman. John and I did some, up on the reservation—you could tie into a twelve-pound rainbow up there now and then—but mostly it was just a way to piss away those long, long winters. We'd joke about cutting troughs long enough to cast a fly into. Drag a streamer across the noses of those gaping trout; how they'd knock themselves out against the bottom of the ice, thinking if they had a Muddler in their mouth, they must need to jump. But we never laughed at it the way some do, never quite got over that quiet, aquarium-eye view of the water and the fish we chased all summer long. Being cramped up over a hole, though, no matter how beautiful a hole, just wasn't getting out, wasn't thrashing through willow to find a spot you'd never seen before, wasn't canoeing through water you knew was tougher than you, scared stiff, but wondering what lay on the other side, what holes and eddies and riffles you'd find if you lived through the ride, me screaming at John to paddle left, or right, or backward, all nonsense because I was scared and we didn't know enough about whitewater, but him letting it roll off because he was as scared, and he knew fear only made me mad.

The ice was all just a side show, a few Saturdays' diversion until the spring opened us up again. No way of guessing it'd one day become the only thing keeping me going.

I give a jig, the hula skirt shimmies, then settles, the leadhead twisting back to the left, steadying. Hell, I'd damn near eat it myself, and I watch it down there in the quiet.

Once, in Idaho, out in the lava flats of the desert, John and I found a pothole lake we'd never even thought to look for on a map. We were chukar hunting, not fishing, but we came back. It was huge, not something unknown, except to us, though really, for all its size, we hardly ever found anyone else there. Just too far from anywhere. Just perfect.

Then, years and years later, after John's first heart attack, the bypass, his move down with Sophie to Phoenix where he had his second and third, I went back alone. In the fall, brought the shotgun, in case the chukars were too much to resist. Geraldine had been gone for years by then, or of course she would have kept me from doing such a fool thing. Me over seventy, trying a float tube for the first time, only because the canoe was getting tough to wrestle on my own, a canoe I used to hoist overhead for a two-mile portage like it was nothing more than a chip for my shoulder.

Once out there, just looking up those vertical ridges of cutting rock, I knew my chukar days were a thing of the past. Locked my shotgun in the case and drove on to the lake. A kidney-shaking two track all the way. A single truck was there, empty, a boat trailer behind it. There was no sign of any boat on the water, but I cursed them anyway.

That pothole—and no, damn it, I'm not telling you its name or where it is; find it yourself, same as me and John—held trout that would make you do fool things for. Reel-stripping dynamos that'd break the water to splash back down like you see those humpbacks on the TV. John and I'd sat gaping in our canoe on more than one occasion, holding dead, limp line between our fingers and staring off into that water where something big had almost happened.

Once I got the float tube contraption figured out enough, got the flippers strapped on and all, I damn near landed on my face till I found out walking backward worked a whole lot better. I waded out then, and the tube came up into my armpits and then I was floating. Kicked out a ways with my big flippers, and couldn't help but laugh out loud. It was like being in the water. Swimming and fishing at the same time.

The desert there is nothing but broken giant sage, mountains all around the north, east, and west, but a long way off. I tell you, it's no place to go looking for a trout hole. And down in that tube, your chin practically touching the water, you lose sight of everything but those mountains pretty fast. Just down too low. Casting took some getting used to too, and I'm not afraid to admit I heard the watery slap of my backcast more than a few times till I got it all figured out.

But good Lord, once I had things lined out, was finally able to twitch a Woolly Bugger down through the depths, I tied into a real one.

Once I realized what I had, and it didn't take long, though he didn't leap, fought instead in head-down, freight-train rushes, brown maybe, I figured, I knew I'd have to chase him down. I found I could paddle that little tube best backward, dolphin kicking, fighting the fish over my shoulder, swimming after him in my tiny little boat just like John and I'd race the canoe after the hefty ones, whoever wasn't hooked up paddling after the cutting line for all we were worth. Almost like having the fish on yourself.

Water lapped over my shoulders a few times, and it had all the chill of an Idaho fall, but now and then I gained on him, kicking like mad and reeling back a little lost line at the same time. I found myself laughing out loud again.

It felt like I swam after that fish all afternoon, like I trailed him from bank to bank, crisscrossing the deeps again and again, but I know it was nothing like that. Me out there doing my dolphin kick. Hadn't been swimming in thirty, maybe forty years. Those aren't everyday muscles. Pretty soon I wasn't laughing anymore. Pretty soon my chest was giving me feelings I wondered if John had felt that first time. The second time. The third. And I wondered if that third time he knew that was it, that this pain was going to be the last thing he ever felt, him who felt so much more than most people get to in a lifetime. Standing in a still new-smelling condominium kitchen in Phoenix, Arizona, his coffee cup shattering on the tiles.

Son of a bitch.

I had to fight the fish with the rod, I knew that. So I stopped my kicking, which really had degraded to not much more than a hopeful flail, and turned round to face that line disappearing into the deep blue. And, as if I'd had my eyes closed, as if the whole world had been behind my back while I chased that fish, I suddenly saw what lay around me.

A sky and a lake both the color of cold lead. Whitecaps. Wasn't thirty seconds and there were hard little pellets of snow striking the water around me, stinging my face. One of those fall squalls coming up out of nowhere. Just like any one of hundreds I'd seen before.

I squinted against it and kept my rod up high, fighting the drag, but the fish seemed to sense something through my new white-knuckling, and it took one more charge down and was gone, the line empty and limp in my hands when I'd started to forget that it had ever been that way, instead of charged with that furious voltage.

I cranked the dead line in and lay the rod across the tube. Waves lapped over it. My wet shoulders were already layered with snow granules. "Thank God for wool," I whispered, something John always said when the weather turned ugly, and I felt that bone-weary weight that sets in just before tackling something hard and bad.

I was pretty much soaked, so I used my arm to spin me around. There was no shore I could see. The mountains, too, were long gone in the snow. I was alone in the middle of a deep, round hole full of white-capped, black water.

I gave a couple kicks, backwards again, and, maybe I was already too tired, wasn't pointing my toes or something, but I felt the give on my right foot, the shifting of the fin. I kicked harder, trying to get my toes back in, and my foot shot through the water, unimpeded by any fin.

I sat for a moment or two, the snow pelting my face. I kicked with my left foot and spun, putting my back to the wind. My tube was no longer a craft, but just a spinning toy.

I glanced all around, everything not black, gray. Snow driven through it. My heart raced, and I whispered, "What now, John?"

Gazing down at my neon-skirted jig, I realize it's been ages since I've given it a bounce. I raise the rod tip a couple of inches. Let it fall. Do it again.

A minute later I'm about to give another twitch and the trout appear. Three of them shoulder to shoulder, all of them big, the biggest I've seen on this lake yet, but of course, the stockers have had another summer's growing. They're all edging twenty inches, except the fish on the right, twenty easy for him. He's got a deformed lip, the corner twisted out a little.

Through my green window in the ice, I can see their every spot, every bony ridge supporting fins, every twitch of tail and turn of head. They cruise by about four inches above my jig. Don't give it a glance.

The trout are already out of my ten-inch circle, and I bounce the jig. A moment later they're back, heading the opposite direction. Again they appear to ignore the jig, its skirt still barely fluttering, but as they swim by, I see their tails already changing direction just before they vanish.

"Don't force it!" I can hear John whispering, can almost smell his sweaty, unwashed hair, the way he was always pushing his head over my hole to peek. I'm all set to twitch the jig, but I hold steady.

It's maybe a full minute before the fish return. They're swimming faster now, the big one with the twisted lip half a foot out in front of his partners. He heads straight for the jig. Leaning over my window, I can see him for maybe a foot, foot and a half before he's at the jig.

He twists his head slightly, then veers off. His tail shake, the big, heavy bodies of his partners sailing past, twist the jig on the line, riffle her skirts. Still I don't twitch.

"Hold on," I can hear John telling me, his words coming fast before I can whisper, "I know what I'm doing!" back at him.

On the return, the big trout has gained another half a foot on the others, swimming faster now, heading straight at the jig. At the last second he veers again and I bounce the jig up.

The dart of his head is so quick, the twist of his big body, the sudden white flash of his open scoop of mouth so sudden, I nearly miss setting the hook, but when I do I know he's got it good, and

I ram the stubby end of my rod down through the hole so the line won't scrape away on the sharp edges of the augered ice. "Hold on?" I crow. "Wouldn't you like to be holding on to this!"

I'm alone. I know this. But I crow anyway.

In that Idaho lake, I'd flailed sporadically before cramping up, before having to slump back down in the waves, let my heart slow. My played-out muscles tremored. The snow came harder, not just a squall, but a front, real weather sliding down from the mountains, something any fool should have seen coming. The sky was dark with it, and with the day's end. I decided to let the wind drive me to whatever shore it would. The wind was out of the west, I guessed, but maybe a northern cold front. Either way, it meant a long hike back to my truck, in neoprene wader feet, not boots. If I hung on that long. The tube was so low it didn't cut much of a profile for the wind to latch on to. Just something heavy for the waves to break over, not push along. I was my own sea anchor.

I fought the fear as best I could, tried not to let it make me cranky and unreasonable. I could almost hear John chuckling over that, saying, "Sure, now that you don't have me to bark at."

And as dusk really did start dropping down on me, I held my head in my hands and apologized to him for that. I started reeling through all the things I had to be sorry for, and the list was not near as short as I would have liked to have believed. It didn't include losing my favorite fly rod, which somewhere along the line had vanished from my float tube.

When the light hit me, I have to admit it did not make me think I was being called up by angels, John or Geraldine, or Gabriel or any of his crowd either. I'd been vaguely aware of the sound of an outboard, hoping I wasn't merely imagining it growing closer. Sheer, blind luck. Not the first time in my life. As the two middle-aged potato farmers hauled me over the gunwale, all I managed to say was, "When I first saw you, I cursed you." I meant their truck, when I'd pulled up, the usual reaction to finding somebody at a favorite spot, but the next day, safe at home after a long drive with the heater on full blast, I got a call from a social worker in Post Falls asking if I wanted to talk, if there was any recent reason for depression in my life. I haven't been able to buy a potato since without marveling at the size of the hearts of those two farmer fishermen. Only a few minutes later, Carolee called, told me she was coming out. That they wanted me to live with them.

Another thing ice fishing lacks is the fly fisherman's prolonged fight. The tough line and stubby rod don't allow for it. In no time I've horsed the big fish through the hole. It turns dicey for a second getting his head straightened to come up first—I haven't had the heart for a gaff since being yanked out here to Minnesota—then he's coming through, when the line parts and he's on his way back down, I lunge.

I catch him in the crook of both arms, staggering back up to my knees, clamping this impossibly large trout in an impossibly small ice house on perhaps the most improbable of lakes, a trophy pond for the new wealth of a generation that's left me behind.

The fish stiffens left against me, then right. It waits then, and I think of myself bobbing in that ridiculous inner tube.

I was ready then, and many are the days since that I have again cursed those good-hearted potato men. I'm still ready now, which, really, is the reason I drag this silly house over the curb and the jogging path and out onto the ice.

Leaning back down over the hole, I slide the trout back in headfirst. It torpedoes off to the side, immediately out of sight, and I don't know if it noses down into the bottom, squeezed too hard, out too long in the foreign air, or if it shoots off with a twist of its tail to sulk and wonder over what in the world has just occurred. I can't see any of that. All I see is the ten-inch-deep, ten-inch-wide circle of glittering clear ice, the still water beneath it, where anything can happen at any second, and where, for me, so much already has.

TROUT WITHIN THE M25

Charles Rangeley-Wilson

The canal curled out of sight. It moved in pulses, the barest hint of a flow, and each pulse tilted a slab of surface, slivers of reflected sky. The sky like dirty steel. Between the canal and some buildings ran a mesh fence, rusted, broken down in places, and beyond were trees whose trunks were black with soot. A couple walked away, she in a green coat, he in a suit, and an older man with white hair that shone hung his head and passed them slowly. Overhead, a jogger ran across a footbridge. I heard monkeys and started walking.

Under the first bridge, a man was sweeping the towpath. The writing on the wall beside him said that Jane gives it to anyone. I asked him if he ever saw fishermen on this canal, and he said that he did from time to time. Beyond him, opposite a striped orange life belt, a cage leant out across the canal, suspended by poles and hawsers, and inside there were monkeys and bright birds, and out-side there were men with camcorders and women with blue hair.

Round the next corner I found Kevin. He was on the far side of the canal where it turned a corner, sitting in a canvas director's

chair, with a 7up bottle beside him and two long fishing poles
leaning out across the water, and right under the point of each
one was a red dot. I stood opposite for a while and watched him
pull up a tiny perch, which he held in a cloth, and after we had
spoken for a few minutes, I walked up the steps to the road
bridge, climbed a fence behind him, and slipped down a steep,
muddy bank until I was next to him on the thin strip of concrete.

"Nah, you'd be 'mazed wot you get in 'ere," he said. "Rand
that corner caught a bloody great perch once. I did. It was one
big bastard. I got it to the edge, an' leant down, I swear I couldn't
get me 'ands rand it, couldn't lift it, an' it slipped back in an' got
off the line. That was guttin'." Kevin looked to his friend a few
yards away as a witness, and he nodded and then shook his head,
affirming the truth and shame of the story.

We sat quietly for a while longer, and then Kevin said,
"Caught a full set of male gen'tals too." His friend said, "Straight
up." "Came floating rand that corner," Kevin pointed to the middle of the canal. "I looked at 'em, and fort they looked bloody
odd, so I cast out, an' hooked 'em. Took a couple of goes, but
when I reeled 'em in, I knew wot they was. So I hung 'em in a
bag off of that fence just there, an' cawled the police. I said I've
caught a full set of male gen'tals out of the canal, an' the copper
laughed an' d'you know what he said? he said, 'Bollocks.' Believed
me 'ventually. They sent divers down, but they never fand the
body, never fand who owned 'em. I was in the paper."

Kevin threw out another ball of groundbait, and a moment
later the red dot dipped, and he lifted the rod like a crane, and
swung another small perch into the bank. "Tiny. Still, we got two
good roach in the net." I asked to see them, and he lifted the net,
hand over hand until water dripped off it onto the concrete, and
there in the bottom lay two roach, each about eight inches long,
gasping in the air.

It was a good place to fish, said Kevin, out of the way, a private little corner. They came down here a few times a week, and

it was their spot. We talked on for a while. He asked what I was doing, and I told him I was just killing some time looking round London, at the rivers and ponds. I told him I always looked for water, wherever I was. He said he did the same.

I said good-bye to them then, climbed back up the bank over some railings and onto a bus to Tottenham Vale. Earlier I'd been to the ponds at Hampstead Heath, and on the way to the Regent's Park canal I'd walked the banks of the Serpentine looking for fish or fishermen. I'd walked the Thames, too, and in all of these places I'd found the serenity of water, there in spite of the fumes, and the sulphur sky, the old condoms, and the graffiti.

From Tottenham Vale I walked to the Walthamstow reservoirs, nine windswept sheets of water within sight of Docklands Towers and zone 2 of the Victoria Line. They are fed by the River Lea, and running from one reservoir to the next as a conduit is the Copper Mill Stream. The short walk from the bus stop to the reservoirs takes you over the River Lea—two branches, one shallow and quick, the other impounded by a lock, converge downstream of the road. Along the railings above the lock were dried flowers caked in a fine film of dirt splashed from the roadside. Some of the clear plastic wrapping was still tied to the railings with ribbons, and so were three grey teddy bears, and a picture of a small boy, laminated in plastic. It was curled away from me, but I could see his smile, posing I think for a school photograph, and he looked the same age as my son. The lock water was dark. There were hundreds of flowers tied to the railings, mostly dead, but some bright and fresh.

The warden at the reservoir looked at me strangely through the thick glass that protected him from anyone who might want to raid the till at gunpoint.

"You just want to look around. What for, mate?"

I told him I'd heard about the grayling in the Copper Mill Stream, and that there were trout in it, too, that had escaped from the stocked reservoirs.

"Grayling have gone, mate. Fuckin' corm'rants ate 'em. If you're a writer, you can write about the corm'rants."

I looked behind him at a glass case on the wall. It held a large rainbow trout, and the writing said, "13lb 2oz, Copper Mill Stream, 1987." I asked about it.

"Been in there a few years, all right, an' I should think there'd be others. I'll tell you about one we caught up in the nets. It weighed fifteen pounds. So we put it into East Warwick, the reservoir down the bottom—that's the club water, Walthamstow Flyfishers. One of those guys is going to get a fright one day. Yeah, those cormorants are bastards. Over in the reservoir, we have to stock trout of three pounds and up so they can't eat 'em. Last year I scared a bird, and as it flapped away, it puked up three trout. You'll see 'em in the middle on the island, like a load of fuckin' undertakers in a tree. Anyway, help yourself."

The Copper Mill Stream ran past the warden's hut and turned under a railway line. I saw a big chub up in the no-fishing zone, lying high in the water, along the edge. It turned with a heavy swirl when it saw me. Downstream, a man in a rain hat was peering into the water. As I approached, he looked up.

"Shame, i'n'it? You had to book to get a swim here. All gone now, you could have it to yerself for a week. Just there I'd see big perch, but they've gone cos there's nuffing to eat. Used to be three hundred thousand roach in here."

I looked at him.

"Not kiddin' mate, best friggin' roach river in the country. Really was. Now all those roach are ten inches of cormorant shit over on that island."

At that he walked off, still looking into the water. I crossed the bridge and walked over to reservoir no. 1. A few yards along the bank, someone was setting a rod down. I asked if he'd had any luck, and he didn't hear me properly.

"You want ticket money? Hang on a minute." He reached into his coat.

"No, I'm not the warden, just wondering if you've caught anything."

"Just startin' up. Nothin' yet, but I've only just got here."

He picked up the rod he'd just put down, and wound in the line.

"That's no good there. You've got to get it right under trees. Right under."

He cast again, the lead flying high and looking to me like it would hit the trees and tangle.

"Still short," he said while the lead was in the air, and it landed with a deep thud, sending up bubbles about fifteen feet off the bank of the island.

"That's close."

"That's not close. You've got to get it close. They swim right along the edge. See that branch? They lie under there, though if you get a take near it from a big boy, you're shagged—he'll go right in there and snap the line."

He cast again.

"No, short again. I need to put on a two-ounce lead in this wind."

He wound in and opened his tackle box, and I knelt down beside him and carried on talking.

"That's a bit of a kit you've got."

"Too right. I only took this up last year. I used to be into match fishing, but I got bored of it. It wasn't a challenge, know what I mean? I'd catch stuff easy. Not bein' funny, but I just caught stuff easy. This carp game is different. You've got to work it out. They're clever. You've got to work it out. It's like chess."

As he changed the weight, I noticed a tattoo on the back of his hand. I wasn't sure, but it looked like two rats copulating, with sweat beads bouncing off the rat on top.

"There's three grand's worth of kit 'ere. Stupid, it really is. That rod rack, cost hundreds of pands. The bite alarm's amazin'. I'll set one up in a minute."

He picked up a jar of bait, pink balls that looked like gob stoppers.

"Pure protein, this, and a smell like a tart's window box. This one's called Tangy Squid. If a carp gets a whiff of that, it'll come from fifty yards off."

He bit one in half, chewed and spat it out.

"Pure protein. Tastes disgustin'. Any runs, mate?"

The fisherman from the next swim down was walking back from the bushes behind us.

"Only in me pants."

"Now watch. We'll sort it now."

He cast the new bait, and it thumped the water just feet from the far shore.

"Now I get the line straight, set it up in this thing, and watch the sky. Carp even breathes near my bait and this alarm goes off. There, pull the line. Mad, isn't it? See, the way it's set up, the hook isn't in the bait. The carp feels the bait, doesn't feel a hook, so he sucks it in, with the hook following after, then he feels it and bolts in panic. Hooks himself."

"Are they big, the carp here?"

"In this one they go up to thirty pands, over there maybe thirty-five, and up the top in Lower Maynard over forty, up to fifty some say. But that's professional stuff up there. You'll fish for a year without a take, you really will. Not for me at all. Those guys bivvy up, and hide after dark, and freeze their bollocks off to catch a big one. Mad, isn't it? Mad."

Further on I heard a bite alarm, and watched as two anglers wrestled with a carp they said was a bit of a minnow. It weighed twelve pounds, and one reluctantly held it for a picture while his mate taunted him. They told me that a thirty-five-pounder came out just a little further along a couple of hours ago. I looked along the length of the bank. It was midweek and there were twenty anglers there, some with tents, some curled up on camp beds in sleeping bags, others brewing tea. All rods pointed at the island in the middle, like siege guns.

Along the path I found a sign with an engraving showing the new reservoirs back in 1884. It was from the *Illustrated London News,* and standing at the right spot, you could find the angle it was drawn from. The scene along this path had hardly changed, though the line of poplar trees was now gone, along with the gentlemen in Victorian clothing, top hats at a jaunty angle. But beyond the reservoirs had been fields and marshes—now there were buildings all around. Walthamstow was a village, a short trip across country from the northeast edge of the city; now it was part of the city—the reservoirs a strip of water in thousands of acres of concrete. Maybe this engraving marked the turning point. The city was belching outwards even as the artist drew the scene. In 1884 there would have been trout in the Lea, but not many, and not for long. The Lea, the Darent, the Wandle, Wey, Chess, Colne, and Mimram—all these spring-fed trout streams were caught up in the creeping concrete and asphalt suburbia.

This death of London's trout streams had got inside my head some time ago. I'd been walking the canal because buried underneath it was a stream called the Tyburn. I'd come up here to Walthamstow because I'd heard about the grayling and escaped trout, and I knew that upriver there was a brook called the Salmon Stream. Now I sat by the edge of the Copper Mill Stream, at the point where the man in the hat used to catch perch. Clear water bubbled through a grill along the edge, and here the weeds seemed particularly bright and alive. As I looked into the water, I thought about the giant rainbow trout that had got fat and been hung on the wall of the warden's hut. I wondered whether I'd ever find a wild brown trout. A black-backed relic between upturned shopping trolleys.

I'd been asking questions. Earlier in the week a guy in the Environment Agency had told me he'd gone to a car park in East

London, at the bottom end of the Ravensbourne River, to the tidal reach called Deptford Creek, and there he'd found two sea trout spawning—one a big four-pound fish. "It's cleaning up, you see," he said. "The Thames is getting better. The Ravensbourne used to be dead. There are dolphins up by Chiswick." I told him that Henry VIII used to keep a polar bear at the Tower and send it to catch salmon in the Thames. "There's salmon, too," he went on. "Some guy called Murphy rang me a while back. He'd caught a salmon on a worm in the River Wandle. In a sewage outfall, in fact."

The River Wandle flows through south London, and was probably where I should have been looking. Catches of huge trout were once commonplace—150 years ago one angler caught three in an afternoon, and all weighed over six pounds. Frederic Halford caught his first two dry-fly trout there, both over three pounds. Forty years later the river was "sage-green and sluggish, a sticky stream soiled by a dozen factories and smelling vilely." It died in 1934, when its last trout was caught by a bait fisherman— a five-pound, two-ounce trout, twenty-two inches long.

Earlsfield station, one stop southwest of Clapham Junction, exits onto a busy street, right underneath the railway line, where the diesel clatter of traffic bounces off darkened bricks and mixes with dank air, ripe with the smell of pigeons. To the south there are a bus stop, a phone box, and a row of shops, some with boarded windows; to the north a garage, then the road curves out of sight, choked by dust and traffic. I checked my map, crossed the road, and turned north, then west past a motorbike repair shop, and just beyond stopped at a small concrete bridge over the River Wandle. Below, the water was clear enough that I could see dark stones and old tyres on the streambed, but there was that tangy, warm smell you can feel on your tongue, and the water was grey, as though someone had been washing socks some way upriver.

From this bridge I could see only a few yards, so I walked back to the main road and headed south to find the Wandle Trail, a footpath that runs up the whole river. Right opposite the station was a tackle shop, and I went in to ask whether there were trout in the Wandle.

The shopkeeper looked at me, not as if I'd asked a mad question, but more like he'd waited a long time for someone to ask it.

"They're in there," said the shopkeeper.

The man on my side of the counter agreed.

"Not many, I don't think, and no one fishes for them. You're not going to fish for them, are you?"

I admitted that I had this idea about catching a wild trout in London, that for some reason the idea had got hold of me. He asked why, and I was embarrassed to give a reason. "I don't know," I said to him, "the world seems so knackered, I just think a wild trout in London would mean that it wasn't." He nodded, and I relaxed and carried on. "Used to be loads, you know. They had a royal warrant on this river, it was so full of trout and salmon."

"I'm sure you're right."

"My mate had one last year," added the customer. "Mostly when they do get caught, they're taken home for breakfast. Up the road the river splits in two, and there's a deep bit by steel pilings. Try a worm along there."

I thanked them, and as I left they both wished me luck.

I found the spot easily, a spit of land with a path worn through nettles, a shallow weir upstream that shelved down to spill foaming water into a dark pool under trees, where the air was cold. Downstream, where the two streams met, bright green weed was anchored to rubbish, and its flowers swayed in the current, while a few yards away Clapham trains clattered over a bridge.

There were dace on the sill of the weir, some rising to small midges buzzing over the water surface. I walked upriver all day,

from Earlsfield up to Carshalton. Through parks and behind factories. I saw a fox. I couldn't find any trout.

I knew of one other place I could try. It would take me more
into suburbia than the city, where the chalk downs were paved,
not so much with office blocks as with patterned tarmac driveways, and superstores. Where the chalk spring water ran municipal fountains, and where the groundwater was replenished each
weekend with soapsuds and road grime.

I got up early and drove out of the city to find the stream. I'd
seen its valley many times, crossing it on a fast dual carriageway.
The first time, I'd noticed a line of poplar trees snaking away from
the road, that we were in a dip, and each time after that I strained
to see past the advertising hoardings that masked the edge of the
road, to catch a glimpse of water. I worked out from a map which
river it was and started at the bottom end, near where it runs into
a major Thames sidestream.

The river ran along the edge of a playing field, and under a
millhouse that had been turned into one of those restaurants
where a guy in a chef's hat carves the meat, and roast potatoes
sweat under ultraviolet lights. Two couples, both ladies large and
talking quickly, both men thin and quiet, watched me from the
lounge as I crossed the lawn and walked into the undergrowth.
There was a worn path that led to a small clearing, the remains of
a fire, old bottles, and mattresses. Beyond was the stream, so
choked in brambles that I couldn't follow it. I had to hack in and
out, peeking into corners. Along the opposite bank, large gardens
ran down from a row of expensive houses, but the fences and wire
made it difficult to follow there, too. A large Alsatian saw me from
its balcony and ran down the garden, barking with insane ferocity,
and inside I saw a curtain flick back and forth. I fought my way
back out, falling out onto the field next to a group of boys playing
football, and they stopped and looked at me, and walked across to
the other goal to carry on their game.

I decided to get back to the car before someone called the police. It took me an hour to find the stream again. The walls and roads and cul-de-sacs of suburbia mask valley contours, and town planners bury rivers when they run across their plans. Eventually I had to ask in a garage, and the man there said I might find it at the garden centre down the hill.

I had to wait to see the manager of the garden centre. He came to the reception area of the office. "So you want to fish for a trout in my river? How do you know there are any there?"

"I don't," I explained. "I'm trying to find one."

"And what will you do when you find it?"

"I hope to catch it, and then put it back."

The receptionist and two office workers had gone quiet now and were listening.

"Why?"

"Would it make sense if I said it was just one of those things I've got to do?"

"No," he replied quite calmly. "No, it wouldn't. I need a better reason. Are you just checking the place out, to bring your mates along? I don't want crowds turning up looking for bloody trout, you know. I know you fishermen, rows of the buggers under umbrellas."

"It won't be like that. Really, it won't. I doubt if there are trout there. If there are, it won't be many. Look, it's just that I've been trying to find a wild trout in London. There used to be loads, you know. All the London rivers were spring-fed trout streams, and now they're all buried, and I'm just trying to find one of them that is still alive, so to speak. Just for the sake of knowing."

"I like fish," he said, suddenly smiling. "Look, I've got fish all over the place." His hand swept along the expanse of fish tanks. "Go on, then. Help yourself. You can stay for an hour, and don't tell anyone you were here."

Outside, a bright-bellied chalk stream chattered through a culvert. Overhead, trucks roared along the main road. From the culvert, the stream split, and one branch ran to a water mill with boarded windows. Downstream, it meandered through an old park, probably once the garden of a big house. Tall oak trees and mown grass. I pulled on my waders.

"Oy! What the fuck do you think you're doin'?" A security guard came toward me from his hut. I could see he'd just put down a mug of coffee.

"It's OK. I've seen the manager. He said it's OK."

"Didn't say nutthin' to me. What you doin'? Goin' fishin'?"

I told him about the trout.

"Yeh, yeh," he said. "Some in there. I fish for carp. See that pond up there? Beauties in there. Trout? Tiny, aren't they? Don't know if they're worth the trouble. But start at the bottom by that tree, if you must." And he went back to his coffee.

So I started at the bottom behind the oak tree, and there upstream I found my trout. I watched it for a while, with the sound of motorway traffic filling the breeze. It flicked side to side over bright stones, and once in a while it would leave the riverbed like a kite suddenly catching the wind, until it hit the surface, and a whorl of water died away downstream. I cast once, and the trout lifted from the gravel, arced back, and hit the fly hard.

UNMEASURED CAVERNS

O. Victor Miller

for Janisse Ray

. . . through wood and dale the sacred river ran,
Then reached the caverns measureless to man,
And sank in tumult to a sunless ocean.

—Coleridge

My GI Bill drained, I returned home to set professional roots in native Georgia soil. I landed my first job at spanking new Darnet Junior College, built smack on top of a swamp where I'd hunted and fished growing up.

Developers had clear-cut the cypress and diverted pure, dark water into muddy holding ponds, hauling in a few hills of red clay to bring the real estate up to sea level. I conjugated verbs and unraveled Romantic poets where in my youth I'd stalked white-tails and jumped wood ducks, where I'd fished barefoot for bass and bream in artesian creeks that meandered through pristine wetlands. I felt the land's transformation as an irrevocable loss but was glad to have a job in an area still charmed by youthful reminiscence and sparsely garnished with a few live oaks and loblolly pines I could almost recognize.

You couldn't have dragged me there with an Allis Chalmers tractor if I'd known that directly beneath my lectern a geologically thin and lacy crust of limestone suspended me a quarter mile over a subterranean lake. When the swamp was healthy, this spongy limestone was saturated and supported by groundwater. But beneath a developed area like a junior college parking lot, diverted rainwater can't replenish the system. Air pockets form in superficial arteries, which collapse into craters that pockmark Mother Earth's complexion and drain her sinuses. By the time Martin Clemency put the piranha in the goldfish pond, Darnet was sitting on a subterranean fundament as insubstantial as a Danish wedding cookie.

I secretly hunted deer in the woods with my bow and my accomplice, Martin Clemency, a five-semester freshman who earned tuition and a small stipend working on the grounds crew. Martin helped me field-dress and smuggle out the venison I poached before my eight o'clock class. We figured the herd, encroached on every side by asphalt and high-rises, needed thinning to prevent malnutrition and preserve some semblance of genetic integrity, and we were right.

I became Martin's informal mentor when I championed his cause to the Committee of Academic Appeals and let him store his bait caster behind my office bookcase next to my bow and five-weight Sage. I liked Martin. Everybody did, except his new boss, Marshal Valentine, the chief supervisor of plant operation and maintenance. Valentine hated Martin, essentially because Martin had too much fun, and it was true that clear distinctions between work and play didn't exist for the boy. With equal zeal he cut grass or chased friends with the riding lawn mower, dug ditches or saluted beauty queens with a backhoe bucket, but the energetic Martin was utterly without malice.

We caught fish, during our noon lunch breaks, from holding inner city ponds that diverted water from the reclaimed wetlands. Martin and Dan Story, a sympathetic coworker, transported them by pickup in a sloshing oil drum of aerated water to Dan's farm pond. Before they took me fishing, I had supposed these mud holes were as lifeless as they were ugly, but under Martin's tutelage, I saw that the shallow bottoms were fanned piebald by spawning bass.

Where did they come from, these fish, these city-limit lunkers? Well, who knows? Were they passed along from progenitors that inhabited the former swamp? Deprived of ancestral spawning grounds, confused younger generations were urged by instincts to migrate upstream through ditches and culverts. Itinerant waterbirds transported zygotic stock that hitchhiked in on leathery shins. A tribute to her awesome powers of restoration, Mother Nature hung in there, latching on to her own as best she could.

Enter Dr. Pietro Cappuccino, a lean and hungry college president in northern migration from central Florida. Immediately after a gaudy installation ceremony, Dr. Cappuccino declared war on the grounds. From plush, airtight office windows in the administration building, dapper thugs delighted in the crack and snap of dozer blade against hardwood. The few trees I thought I recognized from youth were shoved over, exposing roots clabbered with gray limestone mud, waiting to be sawed up, removed, and replaced by grass.

Grass! These bozos cut old-growth water oak and loblolly pine to cultivate centipede grass. They hauled in truckloads of sod grafted in square-foot patches, a hideous quilted pasture with a pharmacopoeia of chemical fertilizers leaching and meandering down to poison the buried wetlands of my youth. "Walking on the grass will kill it," Valentine reminded me as I jaywalked from one parallel sidewalk to another.

I know, asshole. I know.

Did Pietro Cappuccino, in his assault, dream of converting the campus into a gated community? You bet he did. He added golf to the PE curriculum and built a one-hole course with a putting green mowed close as the five o'clock jowls on a Turk. At least sidewalks didn't poison the Floridian Aquifer.

The college recruited more students than the classrooms could hold to justify budgetary requests to build sidewalks. The staff increased geometrically, with new hysterical clerks committed absolutely to meaningless tasks.

But the ultimate blasphemy was the pool garden. In keeping with some perversely biblical notion of pre-Edenic zoological accord, the fountain, pool, and garden representing man's obligation to establish chauvinistic dominion over the creative forces of nature, these idiots created a garden centered by the most vulgar goldfish pond in Dixie, a polyurethane-lined abomination shaped like an amoeba with ornamental water hyacinths clotting the surface. A pulsing fountain of space-age plastic imitating pink marble squirted water dyed blue. The flow and pressure could be hydraulically adjusted to presidential whims. Around the foaming base of this priapic horror, soft-fleshed goldfish wallowed like tadpoles, pop-eyed and arrogant. The icing on the kitsch arrived in a flatbed semi, which toted—I shit you not—two palm trees, burlapped root balls and all, but the president and his henchmen surgically removed the coconuts and cauterized the incision. The president in migration up the eastern seaboard was dragging geography!

"What the *hail* is that?" Martin's mother demanded as she delivered fried pork chops and turnip greens in her son's lunch pail.

The obscene oasis formed a microcosmic contrast to the fang-and-claw free-for-all that broiled where from clandestine deer stands Martin and I harvested inbred bucks with squat necks and corkscrew antlers. Each time I entered the token head of old growth, I returned to my youth and sickened. The garden and its focal-point fountain became for me a potent symbol of waste, greed, stupidity, and loss. Locating it immediately above the most bountiful natural subterranean reservoir in the Southeast was sacrilege equal to crowning the queen mother with a tiara of bottle caps and bike reflectors set in tinfoil.

But I didn't put the piranha in that goddamn goldfish pond. Martin Clemency did. I didn't deny my guilt or conspiratorial implication, in part to protect Martin *in absentia* and in part because I wish to hell I had done it.

Martin slipped the piranha in the inky water—I'm guessing here—to avenge the wasteful death of an eleven-and-a-half-pound female bass named after his mother, Evelyn. The bass was murdered by Martin's boss, Marshal Valentine, the J. Edgar Hoover look-alike who supervised the construction of the unpleasant garden and obscene fountain decreed by Pietro Cappuccino, whose physical presence on campus was, after his inauguration, all but invisible.

Martin and Dan were transporting Evelyn from the holding pond to Dan's farm pond when the aerator in the fifty-five-gallon drum broke. Her oxygen depleted, the bass tilted, frantic gills pumping still water. Martin and Dan were gazing helplessly into the drum, forearms resting on the rim, when old Dr. John Drumble lurched up. The scholarly Drumble, who had never seen a fish out of market cellophane or laboratory formaldehyde, was instantly interested.

In his outsize three-piece tweed, he looked like he'd been tossed headlong and fully clothed into an industrial laundering machine, emerging bewildered, rough-dried, and shrunk. His long, bobbing neck was loosely yoked into a frayed, oversize collar, and his fingertips jangled like bony clappers in the roomy bells of yellowed cuffs. His heels chewed frayed crescents in his overhanging trouser legs as he shuffled across campus like some reluctant early amphibian venturing upon dry land. At graduation ceremonies, John wore his processional regalia like an animated coat hanger.

Martin, realizing his boss would never let him off work to restore Evelyn to open water, dumped her into the goldfish pool while Dan pretended to adjust the pulse of the obscene fountain.

"Pietro wouldn't mind," I lied. "She'll be easy to catch once we get the aerator back in commission. She's only known one hook."

We didn't expect Evelyn to bed in the president's pool, but she did. We figured she'd be easy to catch once she started trying to replace the protein burned up by egg production, but she wasn't. She overcame her maternity malnutrition by slurping up goldfish. I figured she ate her own fry as well, although Martin didn't think so.

But as a symbol of passage, Evelyn's introduction into the goldfish pond marked Martin's departure from my indifferent sway into the tutorial influence of the mild-mannered and highly principled Dr. John Drumble, the only real scholar left at Darnet. Thereafter, when mentor and student passed on the sidewalk or stood together in the garden, the old scholar's attention would bubble up from his deep academic fugue as Martin's goofy grin lured his ruminations from profundity to surface reality. In turn, mere proximity to the bookish old fart sparked rudimentary neurons in the sludge of Martin's brainpan. Divergent polarity charged them both, activating the pure stuff of possibility.

Martin and John were as different as any two people on the planet, yet slumped elbow-to-elbow on the garden bench in the shimmering blue water, their reflections homogenized them into spiritual twins on opposite ends of some wide spectrum of creation where they shared a kinship profounder than mere genetic commonality.

From that remarkable moment, it seemed to me that each of these unlikely *Homo sapiens* had evolved from some mutual chromosomal pattern flung diametrically haywire, or that they were products of original parents who had declined the fruit of knowledge and had tasted instead from the tree of life, entering a brave new world where learning needn't forever be the enemy of innocence and knowledge needn't be marbled with cloudy cynicism and Faustian pride.

John, like Martin, had no notion of toil or diversion. What he studied was whatever captured his immediate interest. His interest now was Martin, whose perpetual lopsided grin approved all that he met, ally or antagonist.

"What does the young swain find so amusing?" Dr. Drumble inquired as we passed Martin at work edging sidewalk fringe with a weed whacker. Martin took a playful swipe at my leg.

"Life," I answered, bolting out of range then readjusting my gait to the good doctor's, "in all its heartbreaking mutability."

Walking with Dr. Drumble required slowing down to a point dangerous to balance. A gyroscopic whirl and jangle of wrists prevented his toppling backward when inertia overcame momentum and he halted like a toy robot snagged on a carpet. His wobbly knees lifted his feet and set them down without purchase, until a companion shoved him back into ambulatory advancement. I watched them on their way to feed their fish. Drumble struggled to maintain momentum while Martin slowed his pace to remain abreast. On inclines, Martin circled his mentor to keep balanced, swooping in when necessary to nudge him free from a muck of inertia. Viewed together, they were cogs in the same bizarre apparatus.

What kept Drumble upright? Superfluous movement, I decided, stabilized him. His jerking arms and neck, his twitching face, his wobbling knees and jangling wrists held him erect when forward motion died altogether.

Then I noticed a resemblance in their movement as well as their physical favor. Both walked like scarecrows strung with rubber bands, ambling preposterously along according to some mysterious dynamic of exaggerated kinetics that propelled Martin and retarded John. The boy marched, cocky as a show pony, with singular electric flair. Kinetic liquefaction rippled through his lanky frame, elbows and knees pumping compounded energy into a baroque style jazzed with excess, yet somehow coordinated. The old scholar, struggling to move at all, advanced like an underpowered Martin with a dysfunctional timing gear. God knows what they talked about. Maybe in exchange for teleological insight, Martin was teaching his mentor how to walk.

"Dr. Drumble laughs like a wind-broke jackass," Martin confided. "I reckon I need to go head-on and take his English Comp I class before he lays down and dies on us. Soon as I get off academic suspension," he added.

"Dr. Drumble laughs?"

But whenever I saw them together in the garden, I sensed and confirmed an additional presence drawn as a by-product into the magnetic equation. . . . The pugnacious face of Martin's boss, Marshal Valentine, peeked around the brick corner. Wide, high cheekbones. A pallid heart framed by caterpillar sideburns. Oily hair raked back from low widow's peak and high forehead.

"I'd be a good teacher," I confided to Martin one day as we returned from a holding pond, "if I knew what Dr. Drumble knows and could translate it to the Martins of the world."

"Do what?"

But by the time Martin put the piranha in the goldfish pond, I had decided that the Martins of the world were better left alone, better protected than domesticated, good for the general morale, especially mine, since academia had become as bland to me as a glop of tepid grits.

––––––––––––

All summer long during his lunch break, Martin fed his bass shiners, which he bought by the dozen, to conserve the president's goldfish or to supplement Evelyn's diet with more traditional fare.

To avoid suspicion (seeding with goldfish was too expensive), he tossed in a handful of brass bolts lest the president, in his rumored (but yet unwitnessed) afternoon walks through the garden, notice a deficiency.

Within a week Martin had Evelyn eating out of his hand. Students gathered to watch him lying on his belly, overhanging the edge, pinching a shiner between index finger and thumb, and slapping the water with his other hand. The bass rushed to the floating moon of the boy's grinning face, sucking shiners from his fingertips into her formidable maw.

Valentine, his face half eclipsed by the brick corner of the fine-arts building, must have figured the boy was admiring his undulating reflection in the disgusting water. Hardly a specimen of ideal manhood, Martin was at least hot from the oven, so to speak, which is to say young, with tawny hair plastered down over spiraling cowlicks at forehead and crown. It seemed to me that Valentine envied him that youth, but maybe the supervisor had more sinister designs for the gangly Martin, more iniquitous than merely finding cause to fire him. It was as though Martin's good humor was a threat to some perfect order Valentine would established in the workplace. Innocence is itself an enemy to order.

What Martin did on his lunch hour was technically his own business, until he got snagged by one of the innumerable rules, which had grown geometrically as new administrators fortified their uselessness with legislative gobbledygook incomprehensible to everybody but themselves. Poor Martin, a product of American education, couldn't read, which stood him in double jeopardy. Policies levied against him had a compounding impact. Moreover, he was the perfect scapegoat to draw the administrators' fire. No bureaucracy could fine tune itself to mechanical infallibility with creatures like Martin in it.

Maybe Valentine plotted also against the old scholar, who balanced himself with spastic jerks beside the prone boy feeding the bass. In spite of, or because of, his considerable learning, John had acquired a kind of singular naïveté akin to innocence, which paired him perfectly with Martin, whose only connection to learning was absolute immunity. John was as astounded by Martin's intellectual innocence as he was fascinated by the fish.

Miraculously, even with the benefit of relentless espionage, Valentine seemed never, in the better part of two semesters, to realize what the boy was up to, his torso extended from the hips over water, arms extended, and his lips mumbling to Evelyn as in prayer. I don't think Valentine was actually aware that an eleven-and-a-half-pound bass lived in the president's fish pond. Utterly without imagination, Valentine was incapable of intuitive conclusions derived even from the most obvious facts. He recognized only what materialized before his squinty eyes as supportable infractions of rules. The real evidence was obscured beneath inky water. The subtle Valentine would never stoop to ask Martin what he was up to every day at lunch.

Increasingly aware that his fish would be happier in Dan's farm pond, Martin was torn between feeding Evelyn and evacuating her from the president's goldfish pool before she caught a fungus or turned blue. He withheld the shiners to starve her enough to swallow one with a hook in it. He spent his days off and late nights fishing for her. She sculled up to his bait, backed away, and sulked. Having forgiven his initial hook, she resolved never to be seduced by man and rod again.

Martin even tried lying on his belly at the edge of the pool, offering a squirming shiner and grasping her jaw as she sipped it in. She indignantly slashed in place, working his knuckles raw, until he howled and turned her loose. Again she pouted, lurking in the indigo water where the last bright goldfish waited to go a slow process through her bowels, their sparkling scales expelled like tiny suns in a cosmic nebula of fish feces.

A fortnight into Evelyn's fast, a terrified wood duck batted pell-mell from the fray east of the playing fields. Apparently confused by tennis court lights, it splashed down to roost in the pool. The hungry bass immediately inhaled it with a smack.

"Hot damn!" exclaimed an evening student rushing in late to English 1102. "They's something living in that goldfish pool. They was this sound like a grease gun sucking a air bubble, and that little hen was *gone!* I ain't never seen nothing to leave this world that sudden."

Finally Martin came to my office milking his cap with both hands. "We got to get her out of there, Mr. Miller. It ain't right."

"We?"

"I can't get her to bite nothing with a hook in it. I've chunked the whole tackle box at her. Live bait, too. Even goldfish."

"You try a duck?"

Martin, incapable of irony, had adopted a moral mandate that the fish named for his mother be restored to the wild before dyed water and an exotic diet corrupted her health and natural integrity beyond redemption. Already she had acquired a paranoia inspired by Martin's stealthy approach.

"Maybe she'll take a fly," he ventured. "She ain't seen a fly. How about you give it a shot with your Sage? I ain't sure where I could catch a duck right now."

A cold snap came through behind a late-autumn thunderstorm, and the weather stayed cold through the Saturday we plotted to bring Evelyn up with a nymph. The physical plant was closed, and except for janitorial and security staff loyal to Martin, the school was closed. I rigged the five-weight with an eight-foot leader and long tippet tinted blue, false-casting enough airborne fly line to present the nymph from a distance well wide of Evelyn's visibility. The fly landed perfectly, triangulated by fountain, willow, and palm.

Numbed by the frigid water, the bass struck with a violence
fueled by outrage and retarded by cold. Hypothermic muscles,
however, slowed her. Feeling the numb tug of the hook, she made
a ponderous and powerful run, crashing in slow motion through
the sapphire surface, erupting a mushroom splash of bluish water
in a single frame of lethargy. She balanced on her tail and shook
sluggishly, more ursine than piscine. Her rattling gills slowed to an
engine knock as she slung bright water beads into the tangerine
sunlight. Spray and bluish water diamonds drifted back to the
boiling water slow as snowflakes. Everything that touched Evelyn,
nature itself, the very molecules of the elements—earth, air, daylight, and water—had fallen under the catalytic sway of her
retarded metabolism. She sounded, glancing off the snotty plastic.
Making a final, ponderous run, she wallowed through syrupy
water, bowing rod and stretching fly line until my tippet popped
with a report like a .22 short. *Ka-pow.*

I turned to Martin and John, shrugging off failure. Catching a
blur of Valentine's face eclipsing behind the brick corner of Fine
Arts, I said, "Aw shit!" retrieving limp line. The guilt of betrayal
washed over me. Carelessness and piscatory ineptitude had sold
out my bucolic pal and his mother's namesake. Valentine's suspi-
cions of something fishy in the presidential pond were confirmed.
Why hadn't I foreseen that Martin's and John's companionship
would attract the inescapable supervisor? But even if I'd antici-
pated him, would it have changed anything? Events by then
seemed to have fallen into the inevitable orbit of a vaster mecha-
nism in which I was an innocent and helpless instrument. Martin
and Evelyn would be cast from the gaudy garden, with mortal
consequences for the fish. Without Martin, John would sink back
into his profound academic dementia. I couldn't know at the time
that the horrible little pond would be the scene of Valentine's ter-
minus as well, the very spot where Mother Earth opened her
leviathan maw and swallowed him whole, digesting him into the

ruminations of her aquatic and limestone bowels. Nor could I know that the supervisor's brief passage through this vale of tears would be memorialized by a gaping sinkhole between Administration and Fine Arts.

I came to work Monday to find an empty pond, the polyurethane sides dulled in a patina of dry scum. Evelyn lay supine in the flotsam of withered hydrilla and bulbous water hyacinth, her white belly bloated in death morbidly suggested the first time we saw her, sassy and full of roe. A dozen fingerling bass were scattered like satellites around her, woven obscenely into a net of hairy hyacinth roots. Evelyn had not eaten her fry, even when denied shiners and forced into fast. A scattering of brass bolts studded the bottom, but no dead goldfish enhanced the carnage that Martin, at least, was spared. When he pranced up to punch in, Valentine met him with a severance check and shouted him off campus. The pool was restocked with prissy, goggle-eyed goldfish, hundreds of them, excess being standard to departmental solutions. More is better.

I didn't see Martin again until the second Saturday morning in May. Through my office window, I saw a loosely strung youth in cowboy boots beside the presidential goldfish pond. I rushed outside, and sure enough, Martin stood gazing into the inky water, a dripping Ziploc freezer bag dangling from gangly fingers. By the time I got to the garden, Dr. Drumble had miraculously materialized. I automatically glanced around for Valentine, who wasn't visible.

"I hate them goldfish," Martin confessed.

"Yeah, me too. Martin, where've you been?"

"They don't belong here." I could tell he'd been drinking.

"Nothing belongs here," I assured him. "I sure don't, and neither do you." It went without saying that Dr. Drumble didn't.

"I mean in Georgia. Goldfish don't belong in Georgia."

"Hmm, speaking of which, what are you doing back on campus? I heard you'd gone to Texas."

"I come home to pick up some stuff and wind up some bidness."

I'd never known Martin to have much business that didn't concern bows or bait casters. We were side by side. I was gazing into the pool because Martin was. "I don't have much juice out in Texas," I began, "but one of the history teachers that left . . . Jesus!" A mushroom cloud of glittering scales boiled to the surface, followed by an orange sunburst and a quick series of minor pyrotechnic explosions like Lilliputian artillery against a deep night sky. "What the hell have you . . . ?"

There was suddenly another explosion of iridescent orts where a goldfish had rested a second before, suspended stupidly in a field of blue. The confetti of glittering scales following an instantaneous reduction to the elemental. Whatever they saw in the spectacle, they found it equally amusing—from Martin's hearty, braying laughter echoed the wheezing hiss of John's emphysemic hilarity.

"Hot damn!" I said as the piranha hit another goldfish. "Wow!"

"Heh, heh, heh," chuckled the crumpled pedant at my elbow.

Martin grinned. "I got to go, Mr. Miller. It's a long way to El Paso."

"Aurora borealis!" bleated Martin's delighted mentor, flapping his baggy sleeves like rudimentary wings.

"Do what?"

"Never mind, Martin," I said, but I too was caught up in the joy of unloosed anarchy in the microcosmic scheme of things.

Martin and John grinned silently at each other, basking in a moment of volatile proximity. Then Martin sauntered off. I lingered at the abominable pond. I had missed Martin in his absence and I'd miss him again, although in the piranha in residence he had donated a hopeful reminder of himself, of the irrepressible integrity of youthful rebellion.

John remained transfixed by the piscine fireworks, his thin limbs swallowed in tweed, jerking in place like a dentist drill caught up in a danse macabre, while an invisible piranha zapped fat goldfish and left trails of glitter through ultramarine blue. At last there was something hopefully sinister in the garden, a seed of apocalypse to oppose in microcosm the gaudy symbol of subdued nature. Little did I know that a far more apocalyptic event than a fish's feeding frenzy moved toward the garden and the goldfish pond.

The evidence of impending catastrophe was there for anyone with sense to see it. Snake holes and sinuses had formed along the outside lip of the pool where rainwater followed the cambered paunch, channeling and eroding gutters between imported earth and polyurethane. It pooled beneath the belly of the goldfish pond, seeping downward into the vacuum of subterranean space. It gnawed the imported clay, natural topsoil and peat, eroding clean through to the porous limestone crust over the ancient, sunless sea geologists call the Floridian Aquifer.

Where fissures surfaced, Valentine poured in yard after yard of concrete, casting thick layers of crust to the swagbellied pool. Erosion ate progressively outward and downward, forming a cast that expanded sincerely as wet cement settled where the water had, immediately beneath the fountain. A subterranean view of the president's goldfish pond at the time Martin chunked in the piranha would have revealed a monolith shaped like a monstrous plumb bob, hanging loose as a tooth in lacy limestone.

The pool was drained again, the discarded water adding new gutters and gorges beneath the garden. A lonely fish the shape of a footprint lay on its side, gasping air and clicking a razor-toothed overbite. Its useless tail fin buzzed and blurred intermittent death throes against the wet polyurethane.

As the president's pond was refilled with heavy water and restocked, Valentine ordered Dan Story to call in another load of concrete, but before the truck could get there, the ground beneath the garden shifted, as the encrusted pool settled a few inches into its wormwood foundation. A wave of blue water sloshed over the rim, and the palms pivoted on undermined balls, slanting obliquely. The phallic fountain shivered, briefly widening its perimeter of foam.

"Bring up the backhoe," Valentine ordered. Then, "What's he doing here?"

Martin and John stood together at the edge of the garden looking on. Nobody had removed the piranha, which glided in stiff, dead circles in the currents of the entering water.

"Hey, Mr. Valentine, I been let off suspension. Dr. Drumble gone to Appeals and got me back in the game."

Drumble chuckled and snorted, wobbling in place. He and I had wrangled seats on the Appeals Committee, and our recommendation that Martin get his old maintenance job back was pending.

The grounds crew attached a cable, and the bucket of the backhoe jerked one tree upright. I thought I felt the ground quiver as Dan Story's sledgehammer pounded a steel rod into the poisonous lawn. He attached a guy wire to hold the palm vertical. Valentine himself stood by the second listing palm, attaching the cable to a sling fashioned from a section of fire hose.

"C'moan back," said the ground guide to the concrete truck driver, who backed the mixer within chute range of the newest dark sinkhole on the pool perimeter. Students gathered. The cable was attached to the second palm.

"Now!" Valentine ordered the backhoe driver.

The warning bells of heavy equipment chimed harmoniously as grout rattled down the chute and the tightened cable raised the second castrate palm, which shook violently as it righted. The instant it reached verticality, it levered open the trapdoor beneath the garden, triggering the tumultuous collapse of pool, fountain, palms, willow, water, piranha, and all—together with Marshal Valentine—into a gaping suckhole, vanishing with a slurp into bottomless oblivion.

Motley spectators fell prostrate upon the shimmying lawn, ducking the lashing cable, barbed like a stingray tail, with the iron spike Dan had driven into the ground. The garden crumbled through the gaping black hole in the desiccated limestone roof of the aquifer, sinking in tumult into a subterranean sea a quarter mile beneath our feet and the imported clay.

Truck and backhoe drivers and their assistants jumped clear, scrambling like scalded cat squirrels up the network of slick bare roots on the face of the new cliff as their equipment slurped into oblivion. The concrete truck tumbled in riding a thick wedge of red clay, the backhoe diving in on a leash behind a palm, which towed it twanging like a banjo string into the bottomless canyon. The garden and fountain disappeared.

Dr. Drumble, overcome by the illusion that he was being sucked into a swirling chasm, windmilled at the rim until his young protégé lurched to the rescue, snatching him back from the cavernous space into which Valentine had disappeared like Captain Ahab tangled in a Gordian backlash of harpoon lines to the heeling mast of his precious palm.

———————————

"Mr. Valentine never liked me much," Martin mumbled, removing his ball cap and saluting the hole, "but I hate he got sucked down yonder with his backhoe and all. He had lots of good qualities couldn't none of the rest of us see, and he was plenty smart.

'Rules is rules' he always said. And that's the truth. Rules *is* rules. He was a good man, too, I bet. Misunderstood is all. Why, given a chance, he . . ."

"Shut up, Martin." I was deeply rattled, in no mood for bucolic eulogizing.

"Death does not sanctify," added the threadbare old scholar, hooking a wire stem of his spectacles back on his ear.

"Do what?"

"The saints are dead, Martin," I translated, "but dying doesn't automatically make you one."

"Saints? Was Mr. Valentine one of them too?" Martin didn't know a saint from a Shriner.

"He was a living son of a bitch," I hissed, "and dying didn't sweeten him up."

"Well then, Doc, you want to go fishing?"

"Fishing." The old bookworm tumbled the word over in his mind, where it seemed to sparkle new vision, lighting his face in a goofy Martinesque grin.

"Sure, they's a holding pond a couple blocks from here where we can stack 'em up like cordwood."

Drumble stretched his neck out about a foot and snorted, as his triangular head wobbled him into ambulation. Martin turned, giving his mentor a head start.

"Come ahead on with us, Mr. Miller," he said, grinning. "I got me a private pond ain't five minutes from here. I just need to get old Dan to tote us over in the pickup." Martin hollered to Dan, waving a ring of bright keys.

FAREWELL GRAYLING

Paul Schullery

The Robert Campbell Bridge crosses the Yukon River on the southeast corner of downtown Whitehorse, a simple enough circumstance to observe, but one whose implications are formidable, even momentous. Whitehorse, at twenty-four thousand people, contains more than two-thirds, and maybe three-quarters, of the entire human population of the Yukon Territory, 186,000 square miles of mostly wild, native landscape. The Yukon River originates some distance south of Whitehorse. One estimate places the Yukon's headwaters—in mountains near the Pacific coast—only fifteen miles from salt water, but when the river flows through Whitehorse, it still has most of two thousand miles to flow before it finally reaches the sea at the western edge of Alaska.

Even if you're from a big Lower Forty-eight state with lots of open country and square mileage, the scale of all this is daunting. The Yukon flows under the Robert Campbell Bridge, a nice, reasonably modern city bridge. From there it heads north and west toward the Alaska line, and then runs the immense width of that state. But from the time it leaves Whitehorse until it reaches the ocean, it only passes under two more bridges, one not far north of Whitehorse, and the other far off in Alaska—the haul road to Prudhoe Bay. It rarely even has a road along it, much less anything like Whitehorse's big stores, hotels, and fast-food places. It is fed through all those hundreds of miles by countless big rivers and small streams, inhabited by countless anonymous fish, living out countless unheralded lives. Here in Whitehorse, the riverbank is as citified as it's ever going to get.

And it's really quite citified. Whitehorse is a splendid, modern town, with well-maintained parks and lots of nice buildings almost up to the water. Just upstream from the bridge, the restored and historic SS *Klondike,* a grand old sternwheeler now open for tours, sits high and dry on the lawn. I'd taken the tour on a previous visit, so while Marsha got in line to hear about the hard life and seamy interpersonal relationships of early Yukon rivermen, I drove over to the Rotary Peace Park, just downstream of the bridge, put my fly rod together, and waded into the river by the boat ramp.

I had been told that there were grayling right in town. This wasn't especially surprising, as I knew any number of towns close to my own home—Bozeman, Missoula, Livingston, Jackson—that had pretty good trout fishing more or less in among the stores and houses. But it was enormously exciting right then, because we were on our way home after two months in the North, and I had almost adjusted to the forlorn reality of losing access to what I considered one of the region's most delightful novelties—roadside grayling. Now suddenly a new last chance appeared. It seemed so improbable that I almost didn't bother, but Marsha insisted, bless her heart. I had an hour; why waste it? (She reinforced this logic with some endearing sentiment, such as "Don't be such a poop! Go fishing!")

I've always admired grayling. I think of them as a fish better suited to an unreachable fantasy landscape than even to the beautiful places I get to fish. That unlikely, lovely dorsal fin and that dainty elegance of form deserve some finer home, perhaps a William Morris riverscape with perfectly circular purple shade trees and palomino unicorns grazing the banks. Having grayling so handy here in the North, rather than the way they are back home, where I can find them only at the end of a long hike to some mountain pond, was a giddy luxury. All along the highways I'd been driving for two months, I could pull over and have a shot at grayling, and each fish, no matter its size, seemed more grand a gift than the last.

But now it was over and we were heading home. I was already missing them, and suddenly here I was with an hour to kill and a river full of grayling allegations right in front of me. That it was the Yukon River itself—the river of Sergeant Preston, Jack London, Pierre Berton, and a crowd of other boyhood enchantments—made realization almost thrilling. But somehow it also increased the odds that I wouldn't be able to buy a fish, which was probably why I needed Marsha's nudge to go fishing at all.

It was raining a little. The river was big and gray and flat and not especially promising, but there was just a crinkle of a break in the current not far out that suggested a submerged shoal. I cast a hare's ear nymph above it and let it swing around.

Grayling, like so many fish in famously distant places, are notoriously easy to catch except when they're not. The wildest, least-educated fish, farthest from the road, farthest from the fly shop, farthest from the nearest witness, can turn on you and devastate your hog-heaven expectations. If I hadn't learned that in many years in the Rockies, I certainly could have learned it again in the Yukon and Alaska that summer as I watched these legendarily naive fish follow my flies around with an exasperating reluctance to take. I watched, remembering all the while the advice of various tackle-shop experts: "This is a good fly pattern for grayling, but it don't really matter, you know—they're just grayling."

So that day in the rain, when I felt the first little hit, and a few casts later, when I hooked the first grayling, I could hardly have been more grateful. Suddenly the whole town—even the incredibly slow traffic light at the corner of Second and Robert Service that begrudged the traffic progress in all directions—seemed a kindly, generous place. Somehow all at once it seemed that this bustling town provided just the kind of send-off a river should before it reverts to the immense wildness the Yukon River was about to embark upon. And it had now provided me with just the kind of send-off I needed, too.

I caught five of these precious fish, maybe eight to eleven inches, in about fifteen minutes. I missed a lot of other hits. Then a couple men in a small motorboat came by and headed in toward the ramp, and the fish stopped feeding. It was enough. I went back to my car and put my light trout gear away for the rest of the trip south to Wyoming. As I took my turn at the glacially paced traffic light, I could hardly stand the wait to tell Marsha about the nice surprise of such willing grayling just when I thought I wouldn't see them again.

We were working our way down to Skagway that day, to catch a ferry to Juneau, but we had time to explore Whitehorse a little more. I insisted on a stop at the shiny new Yukon Beringia Interpretive Centre, a terrific museum full of ancient mammal species—long-extinct creatures that captured my imagination as much as had the grayling. The remnants of the Beringian fauna were another of the Far North's unheralded wonders: along the banks and on the long, shifting bars of these subarctic rivers lay, freshly exposed, the cracked and stained bones of Pleistocene giants. Sergeant Preston hadn't told me the half of it.

Walking among the skeletons of huge ursids and proboscids, I almost hurried right past a small, free-standing exhibit case that contained a flat, slate-colored fossil. But something made me look. The text explained that I was looking at a two-million-year-old grayling, just discovered the year before along the Porcupine River near Old Crow, far to the north.

I think most fishermen would agree that we come by our stories pretty easily. Most days that we're out there, something happens that, if we are called upon, we can shape into a passable narrative, a nice little tale, enjoyable to us and our companions that day, no matter how boring our friends or family might find it later. The fates are generous with these little gifts—these inconsequential yet momentous microdramas in which we either star or make fools of ourselves. We put ourselves out there to have things happen, and we think we know what we want to happen, but the stories that come upon us and take over the narrative are hardly predictable. Afterward, and sometimes even while the story is working itself out, we become aware that this is the part we'll talk about next week, or next year.

But once in a while the fates get really heavy-handed. They lay it on so thick it seems surreal. I don't know whether this is just to remind us of how thoroughly we are not in charge of our fishing lives—or maybe it's the real definition of fisherman's luck. For whatever reason, every now and then the story gets almost too good, and if we didn't know ourselves so well, we'd swear we must be lying about this one. Catching my farewell grayling right there in town, in the Yukon River for heaven's sake, was a nice, well-rounded little episode, a perfectly tolerable and tastefully symmetrical little tale. It wrapped up a magical acquaintance with the fish of a magical summer.

But going right from the river to this museum, and encountering the grandmother of all grayling, a fish that swam these drainages before my ancestors could even say "dorsal fin," was a kind of emotional jackpot—a nature experience of spectacular breadth and depth, especially considering that I still hadn't left town and wasn't even out-of-doors. Stumbling upon that fossil fish right then was the kind of thing that only happens to writers in books I don't really believe, where the narrative seems too convenient, even contrived, like an old episode of Marlin Perkins's

"Wild Kingdom," where rare nocturnal animals constantly wander right in front of Marlin's blind in broad daylight. ("Oh look, Jim, there's another Billinghurst kudu; by the way, did you know they've been extinct since the early Holocene?")

Realizing this made me uneasy, because I had actually been hoping to write a little book about grayling—nothing technical or exhaustive, just a quiet celebration of a lovely creature. If I was a great believer in omens, I could read this day as all the reason I needed to go ahead and write the book, or as all the reason I needed to forget the whole idea.

But whatever I decided about that, it had happened. Even though it wasn't my biggest grayling of the summer, this gray stone profile immediately became my favorite. Fossils, which, despite their temporal distance, seem to me to be more immediate than photographs and more dimensioned and persuasively accurate than sculpture, have more life in them as well. I couldn't get enough of looking at this one. By the time we headed down the road to Skagway, it was a much more memorable catch than the live, squirmy, quick little fish I'd caught that morning.

I pictured it holding along the bank under a leaning spruce, darting up to pull a few ancestral mayflies under the surface. I imagined it dodging whatever sort of megafauna might come thundering through the shallows of its river. And I could see it trustingly swaying beneath a steep clay slope that all at once gave way and trapped it, so flat and perfect, for its two-million-year wait for scientific discovery. I tried to picture the vast, stairstepping line of generations between it and my little Yukon fish that day but pretty much failed. The gap was too big, the connections too tenuous. I finally settled on enjoying it for its fabulous remoteness, several removes beyond the living fish I was just then regretting having to leave behind.

And there I left it, no regrets, no hopes, no needs, beyond being allowed to enjoy it as a personification of nature's memory, a long, faint genetic trail reaching back to a species in its younger and entirely uncelebrated days—when being a fish in a river had no cultural implications, no literary burdens, and only the most spectacularly faint odds of ever coming to the attention of a being who would see it as anything other than a monster or a meal or a mate.

And then just the other day, three years after my previous visit, I was back, attending a conference on the upper Yukon ecosystem in Dawson City, soaking up a world of new information from historians, geologists, archeologists, folklorists, and native people (whose often very nonscientific view of this northern landscape was the most persuasive and satisfying of all).

I talked with one of the speakers, John Storer, one of the region's leading paleontologists, about Beringian fauna. When I mentioned the grayling at the Beringia Centre, he calmly informed me that it had recently been reclassified as a whitefish. It was the mental equivalent of having your line suddenly and unexpectedly go slack. Something very big had just gotten away, and I was pretty disappointed.

But only for a moment. With no effort, and to my considerable surprise, I found myself in a new and perhaps even more entertaining story. Though I've always admired them, whitefish occupy the lowest rung on the sportfishing ladder; in the traditional and somewhat narrow view of most sportsmen, whitefish are as charisma-impaired as a fish can be and still matter at all. Landing one is the trout fisherman's equivalent of the duck hunter mistakenly shooting a coot. Back in Wyoming and Montana, there are always guys catching whitefish and trying to convince themselves (or the rest of us) that they've really caught grayling. And now I had just outdone even those hopeful failures. Not only had I not caught the original grayling, I'd caught the original wrong fish. There was a kind of iconoclastic distinction in this, so I went with it. It didn't feel quite as good as having caught a grayling, but I could live with it.

STONECATS IN THE SUSQUEHANNA

Jon Rounds

I wasn't thrilled about the idea of moving to Harrisburg. As a child growing up in rural Bucks County, north of Philadelphia, my world view was shaped by *Outdoor Life,* and on my mental map, the urban areas of the eastern United States were foul gray wastelands. I caught my first game fish—a largemouth bass—in the Delaware canal on a C.P. Swing when I was nine, and thus became a fisherman for life, one who would ever after rate a place according to its proximity to good fishing and distance from cities and who would not feel connected to a place until he'd established his home waters. By these criteria, my life for the first thirty years seemed to be moving in the right direction. Born in New Jersey, raised in Bucks County, settled in State College, Pennsylvania, deep in the middle of the state.

But then my wife was offered a good job in Harrisburg, and when you are newly wed with a one-year-old son and your own job isn't so promising, you move. We got an apartment in the suburbs, across the river from the city, and I began scouting the local waters. My choices were trout streams, a few lakes, and the Susquehanna.

I started with trout. There are some famous limestone streams in the area, and the Yellow Breeches was closest. I'd drive the back roads, following the stream through the developments and cornfields, find a place to pull off and park, and then wade in cutoffs and sneakers. I used ultralight spinning gear and caught my share of early-season trout on Panther Martins and Rooster Tails. Sometimes I would go to the catch-and-release area near Boiling Springs, a quarter-mile of nice water running through the manicured grounds of Allenberry Resort, with its tennis courts, playhouse, and restaurant. This is where the fly fishermen go. It's heavily fished but heavily stocked, and since the trout are released, there are always plenty of them. And the fishermen are polite. You'll see two or three standing in a pool, discussing whether it's a size 16 or an 18 sulphur the trout are rising to. I got self-conscious using spinning gear at Allenberry and gradually got into fly fishing, which makes the whole deal a lot more interesting. But still, fishing there seemed to me too much like the other activities, the tennis and the lawn bowling. The fact is, all the trout fishing around Harrisburg is pretty tame. You're assured of catching fish within a few weeks of stocking, but the trout are pale and dumb and soon gone.

Toward the middle of the summer I'd sometimes go to Pinchot Lake or Lake Marburg, but there's something municipal about fishing for stocked largemouths in man-made lakes, with their unnatural shorelines, vast concrete dam breasts, roped-off swimming beaches, paddleboat rentals.

I was drawn, then, to smallmouth bass in the Susquehanna, but it was not an easy kind of fishing to get into. The river was daunting, inaccessible, and I didn't have a boat. I drove to Marysville once or twice, parked by the railroad tracks and walked down to the river, but the current there was swift and the rocks slippery, and though I caught a few small bass, wading proved to be too much work for access to too little water.

When I could afford it, I got a fourteen-foot johnboat with a ten-horse outboard and began fishing the Juniata, a lazy river that winds through the rural counties north of Harrisburg and joins the Susquehanna at Duncannon, about ten miles above the city. I'd go out on weekends, put in at one of the public boat ramps between Duncannon and Lewistown, and catch lots of small bass on twister tails and Mepps and Rapalas. Then one evening, pulling the boat out at Amity Hall, I saw a guy with a stringer of a dozen huge smallmouths, the biggest maybe four pounds. My jaw dropped. I asked him where he'd gotten them, hoping—I don't know—that he was from the game commission and had been electro-shocking.

"Oh, up and down here, some in the big river," he said, pointing to the general area I'd just fished and beyond, to the confluence with the Susquehanna a half-mile downstream. I asked what he'd been using. Stonecats, he said.

I'd never heard of a stonecat—some kind of baitfish I assumed—and was still leery of the big river. Across from Harrisburg, the Susquehanna is flat and placid because the Dock Street Dam, at the south end of the city, raises the water level several feet. It's created an ugly stretch of water, a virtual lake where fat people grill hot dogs on pontoon boats and jet-skiers weave in and out of traffic, a lake deep enough for a garish red-and-white paddlewheeler named The Pride of the Susquehanna to cruise up and down, churning the water to a froth.

Above City Island, however, the river is itself—wide, rocky and treacherous. It's a boater's nightmare. You need a shallow draft-boat, and if you use a conventional outboard, you're advised to bolt a steel cage around your prop to protect it from rocks. And though you are still in the greater Harrisburg area, down there on the river, below the highways and the bridges, it is wild. There are egrets and herons and terns and cormorants and acres and acres of smallmouth bass.

It took me a whole summer of boating on the Juniata to feel competent enough to try the Susquehanna. The first place I went was Fort Hunter. This was a mistake. Of all the public access areas within close range—Falmouth, Middletown, City Island, West Fairview, Fort Hunter—the stretch above Fort Hunter is the trickiest to navigate. The ramp itself is on a broad pool just below Dauphin Narrows—no problem putting in and boating there— but the best bass water is upriver, toward the Narrows, right in the middle of a boulder-strewn stretch below the Statue of Liberty, a fifteen-foot-high replica some nut erected on an old bridge pier. From above, on Route 322 or Route 15, this water looks irresistible. You can see where the bass will be—in the pocket water behind the boulders—and there are thousands of boulders. Getting a boat to where the fish are is another matter. It's not the rocks you can see, but those just below the surface that do you in. If they're in swift water and close enough to the surface, they make the telltale **V**. But in relatively flat water or in murky water or in water chopped by the wind, you tend to find them with your lower unit, and after a few trips to Fort Hunter, the blades of my prop looked like someone had been at them with a hammer.

In time, I got up the nerve to try the upper levels, and after some prop banging and cussing, began to get up there regularly. Sure enough, the bass were right where you'd expect them to be, behind the boulders. Most I caught were still small—there'd be days when I'd catch nothing over ten inches—and I began to hear of big bass caught on live bait—helgrammites, shiners . . . and stonecats.

I was determined to try stonecats but couldn't find them anywhere. I bought a minnow bucket and would stop and ask at every bait store I passed. One of them was Rockville Bait, a little shack under the Rockville Railroad Bridge (billed as the longest stone arch railroad bridge in the world). The proprietor was a skinny bearded guy who was always smoking a cigarette. I stopped two or three time over the course of one summer. Each time he'd tell me to try back later in the year.

One October afternoon I was hauling the boat to the Fort Hunter ramp and saw a hand-lettered sign in front of Rockville Bait: STONECATS IN. I pulled over, parked, and carried my minnow bucket into the dark, smoky room. The bait prices were listed on a chalkboard behind the counter, where the guy sat smoking. The stonecats were $1.69.

"The stonecats," I said, pointing up to the sign, "what's that, a dozen, half-dozen?"

He laughed. "That's each."

I made some remark but asked him for a half dozen. He took my bucket into the back room. I heard him cussing. "Sons a bitches. Goddamnit." He came out sucking his finger.

"Man they're riled up this morning. Little bastards tried to get me." (Over the next couple seasons I would find that the little bastards were always trying to get him. I know now that he was just getting jabbed by their pectoral fins when he grabbed them in the tank, but he thought, I guess, they were attacking and stinging him somehow.)

I inspected the stonecats as I tranferred my tackle from the car to the boat at the Fort Hunter ramp that day. They were tiny catfish, about two-and-a-half inches long, a rusty brown color, with flat heads and the stiff, spiny fins I'd first experienced taking bullheads off the hook as a kid.

The afternoon was warm. I took off my jacket and motored slowly up toward the Statue of Liberty. The river was low and clear, as usual for the fall, and it was tough going because my familiar routes didn't have enough water in them to float the boat. I went to the far east bank, cocked the motor up to its highest position, and scraped and bumped my way up a long gravel channel to the second level and began cutting across to the west shore, thinking it might be easier to get around on that side, where there are lots of riffles but fewer big rocks. It took me ten minutes to get across. I cut the motor and dropped anchor below a wide riffle with some water behind it.

I admit to being a little nervous about getting the first stonecat out of the bucket, after the scene at the bait store. I stuck my hand in there, waited till one swam into my cupped palm, and gingerly lifted it out. It squirted out onto the bottom of the boat, where it flopped around until I caught it again and stuck it on the hook.

I lobbed it behind the riffle and let it drift. It twitched enticingly and I held the rod low, waiting for the strike. It was exciting. I was picturing the bass on that guy's stringer at Amity Hall.

Nothing happened on the first drift, so I reeled up and cast again to a different spot. A bump. I lifted the rod to set the hook, but it was just a snag. I jerked free, reeled in, inspected the stonecat—still twitching, the hardy little bugger—and cast a third time. Nothing. I made ten more casts to that spot without getting a hit.

I pulled anchor and drifted down to the next riffle. A long, slow coal train was starting over the Rockville Bridge. An egret stood in the shallows on the near bank, still as a lawn ornament.

On my second cast at the new spot, I snagged a rock and lost the stonecat. Getting a new one out of the bucket, I dropped it and it slid under the boat seat, where I couldn't retrieve it, even by sweeping my rod tip under there. I put another one on the hook and cast it for a half hour without so much as a bump. This was depressing. Halfway through my $1.69 stonecats with nothing to show. Was I fishing them wrong?

I decided to try to reach a spot I knew in the middle of the river, a pool behind two huge rocks, bordered on either side by grass islands. Even in low water, the pool is two or three feet deep, and I'd caught some twelve-inch fish there on a gold Mepps. I headed toward the middle, going slow, bumping rocks here and there, and found the place, swung up to it from behind and slid the bow of the boat up quietly onto one of the grass islands.

The stonecat on my hook was stiff as a board. I put a fresh one on and cast into the chute between the rocks. The stonecat drifted a few feet. Trout sometimes pick up nymphs so delicately that you need a strike indicator—a little tuft of fur or disc of stick-on foam—that twitches at the slightest interruption in the nymph's drift. When a smallmouth bass hits a stonecat, there is no doubt about what has happened. This bass nearly yanked the rod out of my hands, took off down the pool and jumped a foot out of the water. I imagine I didn't breathe for a moment. My drag buzzed as the fish ran in short powerful surges. He jumped twice more. I played him until he was spent, brought him alongside, and lifted him into the boat. He was beautiful. Bronze, barred. I measured him at a little over eighteen inches and guessed his weight at three pounds. I sat there a moment looking at the fish before releasing him. I may have whooped. To this day I can feel the elation.

Incredibly, the stonecat was still alive. I cast it back into the pool and caught another good bass, a little smaller than the first. This one had swallowed the stonecat, so I rebaited and caught a third bass, this one a foot long. Three casts, three good fish. I cast several more times to the pool without a hit, and finally lost my next-to-last stonecat on a rock.

The sun had dipped beneath the ridge on the west bank. There was maybe a half-hour of light left. I was too tired to motor around any more, but knew there was good water between here and the boat ramp. I put the last stonecat on the hook, shoved the boat off the grass island and let the current take it. I cast the stonecat across current, flipped the bail shut, set the rod on the floor, and let the boat drift.

There happened to be an old cigar in my tackle box, one a friend had given me when his first child was born. I dug around and found it, a Phillies Blunt with "It's a Girl" in pink on the wrapper. I lit up and drifted along, smoking the cigar, watching my line, letting my free hand dangle over the side and the river water sluice through my fingers. I could see the headlights of cars and trucks above me on Route 322 and Route 15, and in the distance, the tail end of the coal train going over the Rockville Bridge.

CREDITS

Contributor Biographies

Richard Chiappone teaches fiction at the University of Alaska, Anchorage, and is an editor at *Alaska Quarterly Review*. His short fiction has appeared in *Gray's Sporting Journal, Playboy, Crescent Review, New Virginia Review,* and *Sou'Wester.* He also works as a contractor, and with his wife is building a house on a steelhead stream in the Kenai Peninsula.

Jerry Dennis has earned his living since 1986 writing for publications such as *Sports Afield, Wildlife Conservation, Gray's Sporting Journal,* and *The New York Times.* His nine books include *A Place on the Water, It's Raining Frogs and Fishes, The River Home,* and *From a Wooden Canoe.* He lives with his wife and two sons near Traverse City, Michigan.

Ian Frazier writes essays and other nonfiction and is a Thurber Award–winning humorist. His work appears regularly in *The New Yorker* and *Atlantic Monthly.* His books include *On the Rez , Great Plains, Coyote vs. Acme,* and *The Fish's Eye,* a collection of essays on angling and the outdoors.

Pete Fromm is the author of five story collections, including *King of the Mountain* and *Night Swimmer*. He is a three-time winner of Pacific Northwest Booksellers Awards for his novel *How All This Started*, his story collection *Dry Rain*, and the memoir *Indian Creek Chronicles*. He lives in Great Falls, Montana.

Paul Guernsey is editor-in-chief of *Fly Rod & Reel* and the author of two novels, *Unhallowed Ground* and *Angel Falls*. He lives on a farm in coastal Maine with his wife and two children.

J. H. Hall grew up in a family of commercial fishermen on the Chesapeake Bay and became a doctor, a writer, and an avid sport fisherman. He is the author of two books of stories, *Selling Fish*, and *Paradise: Stories of a Changing Chesapeake*. His work has appeared in *Gray's Sporting Journal*, *Carolina Quarterly*, *North American Review*, and *Fly Rod & Reel*. He lives in Wayne, Maine, where he works as a medical consultant.

Dave Hughes has written more than 25 books on trout fishing and fly tying, including *Trout Flies*, *Essential Trout Flies*, *Wet Flies*, *Western Hatches*, and *American Fly Tying Manual*. He is the editor of *Flyfishing & Tying Journal* and the founding member of Oregon Trout. He lives in Portland, Oregon, with his wife, Masako Tani, and their daughter, Kosumo.

Nick Lyons is the author of seven collections of fly-fishing stories, including *Full Creel: A Nick Lyons Reader*, *Spring Creek*, *My Secret Fishing Life*, and *In Praise of Wild Trout*. His "Seasonable Angler" column ran for 22 years in *Fly Fisherman* . He is former professor of American Literature at Hunter College and the founder of Lyons Press. He lives in New York City with his wife Mari.

O. Victor Miller taught writing at Darton College in Albany, Georgia, before retirement. He is a longtime contributor to *Gray's Sporting Journal*, and his humorous essays on sporting life have been aired on National Public Radio. He is the author of *The Tenderest Touch*, a book of short stories.

Seth Norman has written for many publications, from *The Christian Science Monitor* to *Field and Stream*. In 1991 his feature on corruption in the Oakland Police Department was nominated for a Pulitzer Prize in journalism. He won the Roderick Hair-Brown Award and the Robert Traver Award for short fiction, both in 1998. His *Meanderings of a Fly Fisherman* was named by *Sports Afield* as one of the "Best Sporting Books of 1996." He is a columnist for *Fly Rod & Reel* and *California Fly Fisher*. He lives in Bellingham, Washington.

James Prosek was hailed as "the Audubon of trout" for the watercolors in *Trout: An Illustrated History*, completed when he was 20 years old. He has since published several books that combine his painting and prose, including *Early Love and Brook Trout*, and *The Complete Angler: A Connecticut Yankee Follows in the Footsteps of Walton*. His latest book, *Fishing the 41st Parallel*, due out in January 2003, is about his world travels on the parallel of his home, Easton, Connecticut.

Charles Rangeley-Wilson of Norfolk, England, is a regular contributor to *The Field* magazine and chairman of the Wild Trout Trust. He won the British PPA Award for specialist writer of the year in 2000, and was a finalist for IPC Media writer of the year in 2001. He enjoys catching pike on a fly.

Jon Rounds is an editor and freelance writer. His work has appeared in literary journals, including *Other Voices* and *Tarnhelm*, in which he won first prize for prose, and many periodicals, including *Pennsylvania Angler*. He lives in southcentral Pennsylvania with his wife, Louise, and children, Jamie and Molly.

Art Scheck is the editor of *Saltwater Fly Fishing* as well as a freelance writer and editor. He was previously editor of *American Angler* and *Fly Tyer*. He grew up in New Jersey, where he began fishing at age two, and went on to become a lifelong fisherman. He has tied flies professionally and edited the work of many fly-tying authors. He now lives in South Carolina with his wife, Mary Jo, and daughters Ellie and Amy.

Paul Schullery is a naturalist, fly-fishing historian, and passionate defender of wilderness. His books include *Real Alaska: Finding Our Way in the Wild Country*, *Mountain Time*, *Shupton's Fancy*, *American Fly Fishing: A History*, and *Royal Coachmen: The Lore and Legends of Fly Fishing*. He received an honorary doctorate of letters from Montana State University and The Wallace Stegner Award form the University of Colorado Center of the American West. He lives in Yellowstone Park with his wife, Marcia Karle.